NATHAN EARLY
Phototype from an Automatic Painting. (See page 196.)

TELEPATHY

AND

THE SUBLIMINAL SELF:

RECENT INVESTIGATIONS REGARDING
HYPNOTISM, AUTOMATISM, DREAMS, PHANTASMS,
AND RELATED PHENOMENA

BY

R. OSGOOD MASON, A.M., M.D.

Fellow of the New York Academy of Medicine

**Fredonia Books
Amsterdam, The Netherlands**

Telepathy and the Subliminal Self:
Recent Investigations Regarding Hypnotism,
Automatism, Dreams, Phantasms, and Related
Phenomena

by
R. Osgood Mason

ISBN: 1-4101-0165-7

Copyright © 2003 by Fredonia Books

Reprinted from the 1897 edition

Fredonia Books
Amsterdam, The Netherlands
http://www.fredoniabooks.com

All rights reserved, including the right to reproduce
this book, or portions thereof, in any form.

In order to make original editions of historical works
available to scholars at an economical price, this
facsimile of the original edition of 1897 is
reproduced from the best available copy and has
been digitally enhanced to improve legibility, but the
text remains unaltered to retain historical
authenticity.

follow that they are without use or interest. It is a truism that our western civilization is over-intense and practical; it is materialistic, hard, mechanical; it values nothing, it believes in nothing that cannot be weighed, measured, analyzed, labelled and appraised;—feeling, intuition, aspiration, monitions, glimpses of knowledge that are from within—not external nor distinctly cognizable,—these are all slighted, despised, trampled upon by a supercilious dilettanteism on the one hand and an uninstructed philistinism on the other, and the result has been a development that is abnormal, unsymmetrical, deformed, and tending to disintegration.

To a few, oriental mysticism, to others the hasty deductions of spiritualism, and to many more the supernaturalism of the various religious systems, offer at least a partial, though often exaggerated, antidote to this inherent vice, because they all contemplate a spiritual or at least a transcendental aspect of man's nature in contrast to that which is purely material. But even these partial remedies are not available to all, and they are unsatisfactory to many.

As a basis to a more symmetrical and permanent development, some generally recognized facts relative to the constitution and action of these more subtle forces in our being must be certified; and as an introduction to that work, it is hoped that these studies in the outlying fields of psychology will not be found valueless.

A portion of the papers here presented are republished, much revised, by courtesy of *The New York Times*.

NEW YORK, *October*, 1896.

CONTENTS.

CHAPTER I.

	PAGE
Psychical Research—Telepathy or Thought-Transference	1

CHAPTER II.

Mesmerism and Hypnotism—History and Therapeutic Effects.. 28

CHAPTER III.

Hypnotism—Psychical Aspect.......................... 51

CHAPTER IV.

Lucidity or Clairvoyance.............................. 74

CHAPTER V.

Double or Multiplex Personality....................... 116

CHAPTER VI.

Natural Somnambulism—Hypnotic Somnambulism—Dreams.. 129

CHAPTER VII.

Automatism—Planchette............................... 151

CHAPTER VIII.

Automatic Writing, Drawing and Painting............ 181

CHAPTER IX.

Crystal-gazing.. 198

CHAPTER X.

Phantasms... 224

CHAPTER XI.

Phantasms, Continued... 262

CHAPTER XII.

Conclusions.. 307

CHAPTER I.

PSYCHICAL RESEARCH—TELEPATHY OR THOUGHT-TRANSFERENCE.

THE status of the old-fashioned ghost story has, within the past ten years, perceptibly changed. Formerly, by the credulous generality of people, it was almost universally accepted without reason and without critical examination. It was looked upon as supernatural, and supernatural things were neither to be doubted nor reasoned about, and there the matter ended.

On the other hand, the more learned and scientific, equally without reason or critical examination, utterly repudiated and scorned all alleged facts and occurrences relating to the subject. "We know what the laws of nature are," they said, "and alleged occurrences which go beyond or contravene these laws are upon their face illusions and frauds." And so, with them also, there the matter ended.

In the meantime, while the irreclaimably superstitious and credulous on the one hand, and the unco-scientific and conservative on the other, equally without knowledge and equally without reason, have gone on believing and disbelieving, a large number of people—intelligent, inquiring, quick-witted, and reasonable, some scientific and some unscientific—have come to think seriously regarding unusual occurrences and phenomena, either witnessed or experienced by themselves or related by others, and whose reality they could not doubt, although their relations to ordinary conditions of life were mysterious and occult.

In the investigation of these subjects some new and unfamiliar terms have come into more or less common use. We hear of mind-reading, telepathy, hypnotism, clairvoyance, and psychical research, some of which terms still stand for something mysterious, uncanny, perhaps even supernatural, but they have at least excited interest and inquiry. The subjects which they represent have even permeated general literature; the novelist has made use of this widespread interest in occult subjects and has introduced many of the strange and weird features which they present into his department of literature. Some have made use of this new material without knowledge or taste, merely to excite wonder and attract the vulgar, while others use it philosophically, with knowledge and discrimination, for the purpose of educating their readers in a new and important department of knowledge and thought.

Amongst the more scientific, societies have been formed, reports have been read and published, so that in scientific and literary circles as well as among the unlearned the subject has become one of interest.

The object of these papers will be briefly to tell in connection with my own observations, what is known and what is thought by others who have studied the subject carefully, and especially what has been done by the English Society for Psychical Research and kindred societies.

When an expedition is sent out for the purpose of exploring new and unknown regions, it is often necessary to send forward scouts to obtain some general ideas concerning the nature of the country, its conformation, water-courses, inhabitants, and food supplies. The scouts return and report what they have discovered; their reports are listened to with interest, and upon these reports often depend the movements and success of the whole expedition. It will easily be seen how important it is that the scouts should be intelligent, sharp-witted, courageous and truthful; and it will also be evident that the report of these scouts concerning the new and unknown country is much more valuable than the preconceived opinions of geographers and philosophers, no matter how eminent they may be, who have simply stayed at home, enjoyed their easy-chair, and declared off-hand that the new country was useless and uninhabitable.

The outlying fields of psychology, which are now the subject of psychical research, are comparatively a new and unexplored region, and until within a few years it has been considered a barren and unproductive one, into which it was silly, disreputable, and even dangerous to enter; the region was infested with dream-mongers, spiritualists, clairvoyants, mesmerists, and cranks, and the more vigorously it was shunned the safer would he be who had a reputation of any kind to lose.

Such substantially was the condition of public sentiment, and especially of sentiment in strictly scientific circles, fourteen years ago, when the English Society for Psychical Research came into being. The first movement in the direction of systematic study and exploration in this new field was a preliminary meeting called by Prof. W. F. Barrett, Fellow of the Royal Society of Edinburgh, and a few other gentlemen on Jan. 6, 1882, when the formation of such a society was proposed; and in the following month the society was definitely organized and officers were chosen. The first general meeting for business and listening to reports took place July 17th of the same year.

The persons associated in this society were of the most staid and respectable character, noted for solid sense, and a sufficient number of them for practical work were also trained in scientific methods, and were already eminent in special departments of science.

Prof. Henry Sidgwick, Trinity College, Cambridge, was President; Prof. W. F. Barrett, F. R. S. E., Royal College of Science, Dublin, and Prof. Balfour Stewart, F. R. S., Owens College, Manchester, were Vice-Presidents, and among the members were a large number of well-known names of Fellows of various learned and royal societies, professional men, and members of Parliament, altogether giving character to the society, as well as assuring sensible methods in its work. Among the subjects first taken up for examination and, so far as possible, for experimental study, were the following:—

(1) Thought-transference, or an examination into the nature and extent of any influence which

may be exerted by one mind upon another, apart from any generally recognized mode of perception or communication.

(2) The study of hypnotism and the forms of so-called mesmeric trance.

(3) An investigation of well-authenticated reports regarding apparitions and disturbances in houses reputed to be haunted.

(4) An inquiry into various psychical phenomena commonly called Spiritualistic.

The first report made to the society was concerning thought-reading, or thought-transference, and was a description of various experiments undertaken with a view to determine the question whether one person or one mind can receive impressions or intelligence from another person or mind without communication by word, touch, or sign, or by any means whatsoever apart from the ordinary and recognized methods of perception, or the ordinary channels of communication.

What is meant by thought-transference is perhaps most simply illustrated by the common amusement known as the "willing game"; it is played as follows:—

The person to be influenced or "willed" is sent out of the room; those remaining then agree upon some act which that person is to be willed to accomplish; as, for instance, to take some particular piece of bric-à-brac from a table or cabinet and place it upon the piano, or to find some article which has been purposely hidden. The person to be willed is then brought back into the room; the leader of the game places one hand lightly upon her shoulder or arm, and the whole company think intently upon the act agreed upon in her absence. If the game is successful, the person so willed goes, with more or less promptness, takes the piece of bric-à-brac thought of, and places it upon the piano, as before agreed upon by the company, or she goes with more or less directness and discovers the hidden article. Nervous agitation, excitement, even faintness or actual syncope, are not unusual accompaniments of the effort on the part of the person so willed, circumstances which at least show the unusual character of the performance and also the necessity for caution in conducting it.

If the game is played honestly, as it generally is, the person to be willed, when she returns to the room, is absolutely ignorant of what act she is expected to perform, and the person with whom she is placed in contact does not intentionally give her any clue or information during the progress of the game.

In the more formal experiments the person who is willed is known as the sensitive, subject, or percipient; the person who conducts the experiment is known as the agent or operator. The sensitive is presumed to receive, in some unusual manner, from the minds of the agent and the company, an impression regarding the action to be performed, without communication between them in any ordinary manner.

This is one of the simplest forms of thought-transference; it is, of course, liable to many errors, and is useless as a scientific test.

Bishop, Cumberland, and other mind readers who have exhibited their remarkable powers all over the world, were doubtless sensitives who possessed this power of perception or receiving impressions in a high degree, so that minute objects, such as an ordinary watch-key, hidden in a barrel of rubbish in a cellar and in a distant part of an unfamiliar city, is quickly found, the sensitive being connected with the agent by the slightest contact, or perhaps only by a string or wire.

The question at issue in all these cases is the same, namely, do the sensitives receive their impressions regarding what they have to do from the mind of the agent by some process other than the ordinary means of communication, such as seeing, hearing, or touch; or do they, by the exceeding delicacy of their perception, receive impressions from slight indications unintentionally and unconsciously conveyed to them by the agent through the slight contact which is kept up between them?

The opinion of a majority of scientific persons has been altogether averse to the theory of thought-transference from one mind to another without the aid of the senses and the ordinary means of communication; and they have maintained that intimations of the thing to be done by the sensitive were conveyed by slight muscular movements unconsciously made by the agent and perhaps unconsciously received by the sensitive. To explain, or rather to formulate these cases, Dr. William B. Carpenter, the eminent English physiologist, proposed the theory of "unconscious muscular action" on the part of the agent and "unconscious cerebration" on the part of the sensitive; and his treatment of the whole subject in his "Mental Physiology," which was published twenty years ago, and also in his book on "Mesmerism and Spiritualism," was thought by many to be conclusive against the theory of mind-reading or thought-transference. Especially was this view entertained by the more conservative portion of the various scientific bodies interested in the subject, and also by that large class of people, scientific and otherwise, who save themselves much trouble by taking their opinions ready made.

It was a very easy way of disposing of the matter, so thoroughly scientific, and it did not involve the necessity of studying any new force or getting into trouble with any new laws of mental action; it was simply delightful, and the physiologists rubbed their hands gleefully over the apparent discomfiture of the shallow cranks who imagined they had discovered something new. There was only one troublesome circumstance about the whole affair. It was this: that cases were every now and then making their appearance which absolutely refused to be explained by the new theory of Dr. Carpenter, and the only way of disposing of these troublesome cases was to declare that the people who observed them did not know how to observe, and did not see what they thought they saw.

This was the state of the question, and this the way in which it was generally regarded, when it was taken up for investigation by the Society for Psychical Research.

Experiments on the subject of thought-transference fall naturally into four classes :

(1) Those where some prearranged action is accomplished, personal contact being maintained between the operator and the sensitive.

(2) Similar performances where there is no contact whatever.

(3) Where a name, number, object, or card is guessed or perceived and expressed by speech or writing without any perceptible means of obtaining intelligence by the senses or through any of the ordinary channels of communication.

(4) Where the same ideas have occurred or the same impressions have been conveyed at the same moment to the minds of two or more persons widely separated from each other.

The first and second of these classes are simply examples of the "willing game" carried on under more strict conditions, but they are not counted as of special value on account of the possibility of information being conveyed when contact is permitted, and by means of slight signals, mere movements of the eye, finger, or lip, which might quickly be seized upon and interpreted by the sensitive, even when there was no actual contact. The third and fourth class, however, seem to exclude these and all other ordinary or recognizable means of communication.

The following are examples of the third class, namely, where some object, number, name, or card has been guessed or perceived without the aid of the senses, and without any of the ordinary means of communication between the operator and the subject.

The first experiments here reported were made in the family of a clergyman, by himself, together with his five daughters, ranging from ten to seventeen years of age, all thoroughly healthy persons, and without any peculiar nervous development. The daughters and sometimes, also, a young maid-servant, were the sensitives, and the clergyman, when alone with his family, acted as agent. The test experiments made in this family were conducted by two competent and well-qualified observers, members of the society, and no member of the family was permitted to know the word, name, or object selected, except that the child chosen to act as sensitive was told to what class the object belonged; for instance, whether it was a number, card, or name of some person or place.

The child was then sent out of the room and kept under observation while the test object was agreed upon, and was then recalled by one of the experimenters; and while giving her answers she "stood near the door with downcast eyes," and often with her back to the company. The experiments were conducted in perfect silence excepting the child's answer and the "right" or "wrong" of the agent.

It has been charged that these children, later, were caught signalling during the experiments. This is true by their own confession, but it is also true that there was no signalling during the earlier experiments, also that the signalling when used did not improve the results, and furthermore that after they began signalling the effort to keep the mind consciously active and acute during their trials injured the passive condition necessary for success, and eventually destroyed their sensitiveness and thought-reading power altogether.

Besides, most of the tests were made when only the one child was in the room, and, as will be noticed, many of the tests were of such a nature that signalling would be out of the question, especially with their little experience and clumsy code.

The following results were obtained, the name of the object agreed upon being given in italics:—

A white-handled penknife. Was named and color given on the first trial. *A box of almonds.*

Named correctly. *A three-penny piece.* Failed. *A box of chocolate.* A button box. *A penknife, hidden.* Failed to state where it was.

Trial with cards, to be named :—

Two of clubs. Right. *Seven of diamonds.* Right. *Four of spades.* Failed. *Four of hearts.* Right. *King of hearts.* Right. *Two of diamonds.* Right. *Ace of hearts.* Right. *Nine of spades.* Right. *Five of diamonds.* Four of diamonds (wrong); then four of hearts, (wrong); then five of diamonds, which was right on the third trial. *Two of spades.* Right. *Eight of diamonds.* Wrong. *Ace of diamonds.* Wrong. *Three of hearts.* Right. *Four of clubs.* Wrong. *Ace of spades.* Wrong.

The following results were obtained with fictitious names :—

William Stubbs. Right. *Eliza Holmes.* Eliza H. *Isaac Harding.* Right. *Sophia Shaw.* Right. *Hester Willis.* Cassandra—then Hester Wilson. *John Jones.* Right. *Timothy Taylor.* Tom, then Timothy Taylor. *Esther Ogle.* Right. *Arthur Higgins.* Right. *Alfred Henderson.* Right. *Amy Frogmore.* Amy Freemore, then Amy Frogmore. *Albert Snelgrove.* Albert Singrore, then Albert Grover.

On another occasion the following result was obtained with cards, Mary, the eldest daughter, being the percipient: In thirty-one successive trials the first only was an entire failure, six of spades being given in answer for the eight of spades. Of the remaining thirty consecutive trials, in seventeen the card was correctly named on the first attempt, nine on the second, and four on the third.

It should here be observed, that according to the calculus of probabilities, the chances that an ordinary guesser would be correct in his guess on the first trial is, in cards, of course, one in fifty-one, but in these trials, numbering 382 in all, and extending over six days, the average was one in three, and second and third guesses being allowed the successes were more than one in two, almost two in three.

The chances against guessing the card correctly five times in succession are more than 1,000,000 to 1, and against this happening eight times in succession are more than 142,000,000 to 1, yet the former happened several times and the latter twice—once with cards and once with fictitious names, the chances against success in the latter case being almost incalculable.

The following experiments were also made among many others, Miss Maud Creery being the percipient:—

"(1) What town have we thought of? A. Buxton: which was correct.

"(2) What town have we thought of? A. Derby. What part did you think of first? A. Railway station. (So did I.) What next? A. The market-place. (So did I.)

"(3) What town have we thought of? A. Something commencing with L. (Pause of a minute.) Lincoln. (Correct.)

"(4) What town have we thought of? A. Fairfield. What part did you think of first? A. The road to it. (So did I.) What next? A. The triangular green behind the Bull's Head Inn. (So did I.)"

In seeking an explanation for these remarkable results coincidence and chance may, it would seem, be utterly excluded. Touch and hearing must also be excluded, since the guesser did not come in contact with any person during the experiments, and they were conducted in perfect silence excepting the answers of the percipient or the "yes" or "no" of the agent.

We have left, then, only the unconscious indications which might possibly be given by look, movement of a finger, lip, or muscle by persons who were present especially on account of their desire and ability to detect any such communication, and on account of their ability to avoid giving information in any such manner themselves.

It seems, in fact, quite incredible that information thus conveyed could be sufficient to affect the result in so large a number of experiments, especially where the experiments included the names of places and fictitious names of persons. Even where signalling is successfully carried on, as, for instance, in stage tricks, it is a regular feat of memory accomplished between two people who have studied and practised it assiduously for a long time, while here were simply children, brought in contact, without rehearsal, with strangers, whose object it was to detect the trick if any were practised among them.

We are forced, then, to the conclusion that the knowledge which these sensitives exhibited concerning the objects, names, or cards which were given them as tests, did not come to them by any ordinary sense of perception obtained either legitimately or by trick, but came to them directly from the minds of other persons acting as agents and striving to impress them, and that this knowledge or these impressions were received by some means other than through the ordinary channels of communication.

Another method of demonstrating thought-transference which should be mentioned here, is by means of diagrams. The experiment may be made as follows:—The percipient, being blindfolded, is seated at a table with his back to the operator, without contact and in perfect silence. A diagram—for instance, a circle with a cross in the centre—is distinctly drawn by a third person and so held as to be in full view of the operator, who looks at it in silence, steadily and with concentrated attention.

The impression made by the diagram upon the mind of the operator is gradually perceived by the percipient, who, after a time varying from a few seconds to several minutes, declares himself ready. The bandages are then removed from his eyes, and to the best of his ability he draws the impression which came to him while blindfolded. The results have varied in accuracy, very much as did the results in the experiments with objects and cards already described.

The following diagrams are from drawings and reproductions made in the manner just described. They are from the proceedings of the Society for Psychical Research, and were the result of experiments made by Mr. Malcolm Guthrie and Mr. James Birchall, two prominent and cultivated citizens of Liverpool, together with three or four

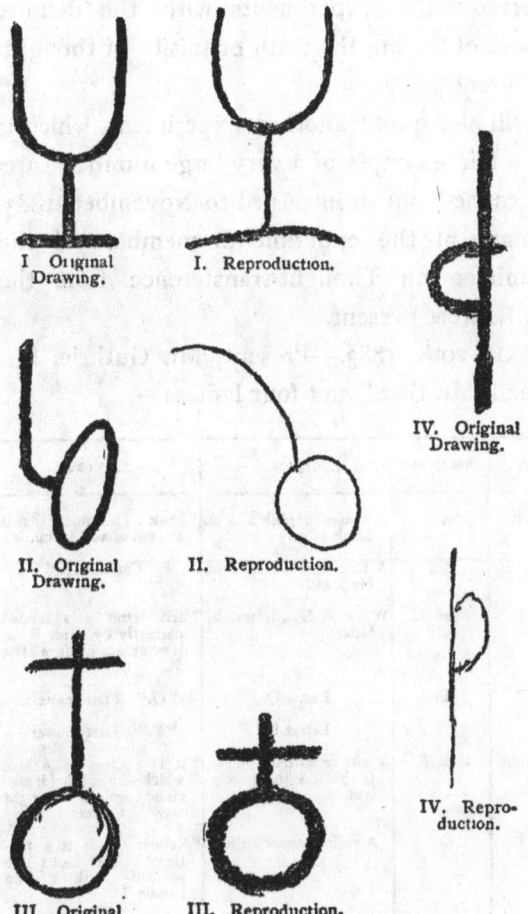

ladies, personal friends of theirs, all of whom undertook the experiments with the definite purpose of testing the truth or falsity of thought-transference.

I will also quote another experiment, which is only a fair example of a very large number, carefully carried out from April to November, 1883. In many of the experiments members of the Committee on Thought-transference from the S. P. R. were present.

APRIL 20th, 1883.—Present, Mr. Guthrie, Mr. Birchall, Mr. Steel, and four ladies:—

AGENT.	PERCIPIENT	OBJECT.	RESULT.
Mrs. E.	Miss R.	A square of pink silk on black satin.	"Pink ... Square" Answered almost instantly.
do.	do.	A ring of white silk on black satin	"Can't see it."
Miss R.	Miss E.	Word R E S, letter by letter.	Each letter was named correctly by Miss E as it was placed before Miss R.
do.	do.	Letter Q.	"Q." First answer.
do.	do	Letter F.	"F." First answer
All present.	Miss R.	A gilt cross held by Mr G. behind the percipient.	"It is a cross" Asked, which way is it held, percipient replied, "The right way." Correct.
do.	do.	A yellow paper knife.	"Yellow ... is it a feather? ... It looks like a knife with a thin handle"
do.	do.	A pair of scissors standing open and upright.	"It is silver ... No, it is steel ... It is a pair of scissors standing upright"

Success was different on different occasions, but this represents an ordinary series of experiments at one sitting. In these experiments with objects, the percipient was blindfolded and the object moreover was kept out of range of vision. In some experiments slight contact was permitted, and in some it was not, but it was found that contact had little if any effect upon the result.

Remarkable success was also obtained in the transference of sensation, such as taste, smell, or pain, while the percipient was in a normal condition, that is, not hypnotized.

The following is an average example of the transference of taste:—

The tasters, Mr. Guthrie (M. G.), Mr. Gurney (E. G.), and Mr. Myers (M.). The percipients were two young ladies in Mr. Guthrie's employ.

SEPT. 3, 1883.

TASTERS	PERCIPIENT	SUBSTANCE.	ANSWER GIVEN.
E G & M	E.	Worcestershire Sauce.	"Worcestershire Sauce"
M G.	R.	"	"Vinegar."
E. G. & M.	E.	Port wine.	"Between eau de Cologne and beer"
M. G	R.	"	"Raspberry Vinegar."
E. G & M.	E.	Bitter aloes.	"Horrible and bitter."
M. G.	R.	Alum.	"A taste of ink—of iron—of vinegar I feel it on my lips—it is as though I had been eating alum"

Some very striking experiments were made by Mr. J. W. Smith of Brunswick Place, Leeds, as agent, and his sister Kate as percipient. Their success with diagrams fully equalled those already given, and with objects the results have seldom been equalled. The following trials were made March 11th, 1884. The intelligence and good faith of the participants is undoubted.

Agent: J. W. Smith.   Percipient: Kate Smith.

Object selected.	Named.
Figure 8.	Correct first time.
Figure 5.	" " "
Black cross on white ground.	" " "
Color blue.	" " "
Cipher (o).	" " "

Pair of Scissors.—Percipient was not told what (i. e. what form of experiment, figure, color or object) was to be next—but carefully and without noise a pair of scissors was placed on white ground, and in about one minute and a half she exclaimed: "Scissors!"

The number of facts and experiments bearing upon this division of our subject is well-nigh inexhaustible; those already presented will serve as illustrations and will also show upon what sort of evidence is founded the probability that perceptions and impressions are really conveyed from one mind to another in some other manner than by the ordinary and recognized methods of communication.

It remains to give one or two illustrations of the fourth division of the subject, namely, where similar thoughts have simultaneously occurred, or similar impressions have been made upon the minds of persons at a distance from each other without any known method of communication between them.

The first case was received and examined by the society in the summer of 1885. One of the percipients writes as follows:—

"My sister-in-law, Sarah Eustance, of Stretton, was lying sick unto death, and my wife had gone over there from Lawton Chapel (twelve or thirteen miles off) to see and tend her in her last moments. On the night before her death I was sleeping at home alone, and, awaking, I heard a voice distinctly call me.

"Thinking it was my niece Rosanna, the only other occupant of the house, I went to her room and found her awake and nervous. I asked her whether she had called me. She answered: 'No; but something awoke me, when I heard some one calling.' On my wife returning home after her sister's death she told me how anxious her sister had been to see me, craving for me to be sent for, and saying, 'Oh, how I want to see Done once more!'" and soon after became speechless. But the curious part was that, about the same time that she was 'craving,' I and my niece heard the call."

In answer to a letter of inquiry he further writes:—

"My wife, who went from Lawton that particular Sunday to see her sister, will testify, that as she attended upon her (after the departure of the minister) during the night, she was asking and craving for me, repeatedly saying, 'Oh, I wish I could see Uncle Done and Rosie once more before I go!' and soon after she became unconscious, or at least ceased speaking, and died the next day, of which fact I was not aware until my wife returned on the evening of the Fourth of July."

Mrs. Sewill, the Rosie referred to, writes as follows:—

"I was awakened suddenly, without apparent cause, and heard a voice calling me distinctly, thus: 'Rosie, Rosie, Rosie.' "We (my uncle and myself) were the only occupants of the house that night, aunt being away attending upon her sister. I never was called before or since."

The second case is reported by a medical man of excellent reputation to whom the incident was related by both Lady G. and her sister, the percipients in the case. It is as follows:—

"Lady G. and her sister had been spending the evening with their mother, who was in her usual health and spirits when they left her. In the middle of the night the sister awoke in a fright and said to her husband: 'I must go to my mother at once; do order the carriage. I am sure she is taken ill.' The husband, after trying in vain to convince his wife that it was only a fancy, ordered the carriage. As she was approaching her mother's house, where two roads meet, she saw Lady G.'s carriage approaching. As soon as they met, each asked the other why she was there at that unseasonable hour, and both made the same reply:—

'I could not sleep, feeling sure my mother was ill, and so I came to see.' As they came in sight of the house they saw their mother's confidential maid at the door, who told them, when they arrived, that their mother had been taken suddenly ill and was dying, and that she had expressed an earnest wish to see her daughters."

The reporter adds:—

"The mother was a lady of strong will and always had a great influence over her daughters."

Many well-authenticated instances of a similar character could be cited, but the above are sufficient for illustration, which is the object here chiefly in view, and other facts still further illustrating this division of the subject will appear in other relations.

The foregoing facts and experiments are sufficient to indicate what is understood by thought-transference, or telepathy, and also to indicate what might be called the skirmishing ground between the class of psychologists represented by the active workers in the Society for Psychical Research and kindred societies on the one hand, and the conservative scientists, mostly physiologists, who are incredulous of any action of the the mind for which they cannot find an appropriate organ and a proper method, on the other.

It is not claimed that thought-transference as here set forth is established beyond all possibility of doubt or cavil, especially from those who choose to remain ignorant of the facts, but only that its facts are solid and their interpretation reasonable, and that thought-transference has now the same claim to acceptance by well-informed people that many of the now accepted facts in physical science had in its early days of growth and development.

The reality of thought-transference being once established, a vast field for investigation is opened up ; a new law, as it were, is discovered ; and how far-reaching and important its influence and bearing may be upon alleged facts and phenomena which heretofore have been disbelieved, or set down as chance occurrences, or explained away as hallucinations, is at present the interesting study of the experimental psychologist.

CHAPTER II.

MESMERISM AND HYPNOTISM—HISTORY AND THERAPEUTIC EFFECTS.

No department of psychical research is at present exciting so widespread an interest as that which is known under the name of Hypnotism; and inquiries are constantly made by those to whom the subject is new, regarding its nature and effects, and also how, if at all, it differs from the mesmerism and animal magnetism of many years ago.

Unfortunately, these questions are more easily asked than answered, and well-informed persons, and even those considered experts in the subject, would doubtless give different and perhaps opposing answers to them. A short historical sketch may help in forming an opinion.

From the remotest periods of human history to the present time, certain peculiar and unusual conditions of mind, sometimes associated with abnormal conditions of body, have been observed, during which unusual conditions, words have unconsciously been spoken, sometimes seemingly meaningless, but sometimes conveying knowledge of events at that moment taking place at a distance, sometimes foretelling future events, and sometimes words of warning, instruction, or command.

The Egyptians and Assyrians had their magi, the Greeks and Romans their oracles, the Hebrews their seers and prophets, every great religion its inspired teachers, and every savage nation had, under some name, its seer or medicine-man.

Socrates had his dæmon, Joan of Arc her voices and visions, the Highlanders their second sight, Spiritualists their mediums and "controls." Even Sitting Bull had his vision in which he foresaw the approach and destruction of Custer's army.

Until a little more than a hundred years ago all persons affected in any of these unusual ways were supposed to be endowed with some sort of supernatural power, or to be under external and supernatural influence, either divine or satanic.

About 1773 Mesmer, an educated German physician, philosopher, and mystic, commenced the practice of curing disease by means of magnets passed over the affected parts and over the body of the patient from head to foot. Afterward seeing Gassner, a Swabian priest, curing his patients by command, and applying his hands to the affected parts, he discarded his magnets, concluding that the healing power or influence was not in them, but in himself; and he called that influence animal magnetism.

Mesmer also found that a certain proportion of his patients went into a sleep more or less profound under his manipulations, during which somnambulism, or sleep-walking, appeared. But Mesmer's chief personal interest lay in certain theories regarding the nature of the newly-discovered power or agent, and in its therapeutic effects; his theories, however, were not understood nor appreciated by the physicians of his time, and his cures were looked upon by them as being simply quackery.

Nevertheless, it was he who first took the whole subject of these abnormal or supranormal conditions out of the domain of the supernatural, and in attempting to show their relation to natural forces he placed them in the domain of nature as proper subjects of rational study and investigation; and for this, at least, Mesmer should be honored.

Under Mesmer's pupil, the Marquis de Puysegur, the facts and methods relating to the magnetic sleep and magnetic cures were more carefully observed and more fully published. Then followed Petetin, Husson, and Dupotet, Elliotson in England and Esdaile in India. So from Mesmer in 1773 to Dupotet and Elliotson in 1838 we have the period of the "early mesmerists."

During this period the hypnotic sleep was induced by means of passes, the operators never for a moment doubting that the influence which produced sleep was a power of some sort proceeding from themselves and producing its effect upon the patient.

In addition to the condition of sleep or lethargy, the following conditions were well known to the "early mesmerists"; somnambulism, or sleepwalking, catalepsy, anæsthesia, and amnesia, or absence of all knowledge of what transpired during the sleep. Suggestion during sleep was also made use of, and was even then proposed as an agent in education and in the cure of vice.

This was the condition of the subject in 1842, when Braid, an English surgeon, made some new and interesting experiments. He showed that the so-called mesmeric sleep could be produced in some patients by other processes than those used by the early mesmerists; especially could this be accomplished by having the patient gaze steadily at a fixed brilliant object or point, without resorting to passes or manipulations of any kind.

He introduced the word hypnotism, which has since been generally adopted; he also proposed some new theories relating to the nature of the hypnotic sleep, regarding it as a "profound nervous change," and he still further developed the idea and use of suggestion. Otherwise no important changes were made by him in the status of the subject. It was not looked upon with favor by the profession generally, and its advocates were for the most part still considered as cranks and persons whose scientific and professional standing and character were not above suspicion.

The period of twenty-five years from 1850 to 1875, was a sort of occultation of hypnotism. Braidism suffered nearly the same fate as mesmerism—it was neglected and tabooed. A few capable and honest men, like Liébeault of Nancy and Azam of Bordeaux, worked on, and from time to time published their observations; but for the most part these workers were neglected and even scorned.

To acknowledge one's belief in animal magnetism or hypnotism was bad form, and he who did it must be content to suffer a certain degree of both social and professional ostracism. The field was given over to town-hall lectures on mesmerism, by "professors" whose titles were printed in quotation marks even by the local papers which recorded their exploits.

But a change was about to be inaugurated. In 1877 Prof. Charcot, then one of the most scientific, most widely-known, and most highly-esteemed of living physicians, not only in France but in all the world, was appointed, with two colleagues, to investigate the treatment of hysteria by means of metallic disks—a subject which was then attracting the attention of the medical profession in France.

So, curiously enough, it happened that Charcot commenced exactly where Mesmer had commenced a hundred years before. He experimented upon hysterical patients in his wards at La Salpêtrière, and, as a result, he rediscovered mesmerism under the name of hypnotism, just a century after it had been discovered by Mesmer and disowned by the French Academy.

But Charcot, after having satisfied himself by his experiments, did not hesitate to announce his full belief in the facts and phenomena of hypnotism, and that was sufficient to rehabilitate the long-neglected subject. The attention of the scientific world was at once turned toward it, it became a legitimate subject of study, and hypnotism at once became respectable. From that time to the present it has formed one of the most conspicuous and interesting subjects of psychical study; it has become to psychology what determining the value of a single character is to reading an ancient inscription in a lost or unknown language—it is a bit of the unknown expressed in terms of the known and helps to furnish clues to still greater discoveries.

With the scientific interest in hypnotism which was brought about through the great name and influence of Charcot, all doubt concerning the reality of the phenomena which it presents disappeared. Hypnotism was a fact and had come to stay.

Charcot, who conducted his experiments chiefly among nervous or hysterical patients, looked upon the hypnotic condition as a disease, and considered the phenomena presented by hypnotic subjects as akin to hysteria. In addition to the method of producing the hypnotic condition used by Braid, he used, among others, what he called "massive stimulation," which consisted in first fully absorbing the subject's attention and then producing a shock by the loud sounding of a concealed gong, or the sudden display or sudden withdrawal of an electric light. By this means hysterical subjects were often thrown into a condition of catalepsy, from which somnambulism and other hypnotic phenomena were sometimes deduced.

I have myself seen nervous patients thrown into the cataleptic state by the "massive stimulation" of a huge truck passing by, loaded with clanging rails or building iron, or by other sudden shock, but I did not consider the process therapeutic nor in any way useful to the patient. Indeed, I have considered the present method of transporting those beams and rails of iron through our streets and past our dwellings, without the slightest attempt to modify their shocking din and clangor, a piece of savagery which should at once be made the subject of special legislation looking to the prompt punishment of the perpetrators of the outrage.

As a matter of fact, neither the methods employed, the psychical conditions induced, nor the therapeutic effects attained at La Salpêtrière, where most of these experiments were at that time carried on, were such as to particularly commend themselves to students of psychology. Nevertheless the great name and approval of Charcot served to command for hypnotism the attention and the favorable consideration of the scientific world.

Soon after the experiments of Charcot and his associates in Paris were published, Prof. Bernheim commenced a most thorough and important study of the subject in the wards of the hospital at Nancy. These studies were made, not upon persons who were already subjects of nervous disease, as was the case with Charcot's patients, but, on the contrary, upon those whose nervous condition was perfectly normal, and even upon those whose general health was perfect.

The result of Bernheim's experiments proved that a very large percentage of all persons, sick or well, could be put into the hypnotic condition. He claimed that suggestion was the great factor and influence, both in bringing about the condition, and also in the mental phenomena observed, and the cures which were accomplished.

He claimed, moreover, that the hypnotic sleep did not differ from ordinary sleep, and that no magnetism nor other personal element, influence, or force entered in any way into the process—it was all the power and influence of suggestion.

Four distinct and important periods then are found in the history of hypnotism:

First, the period of the early mesmerists, extending from the time of Mesmer, 1773, until that of Braid, 1842—nearly seventy years—during which the theory of animal magnetism, or of some actual force or subtle influence proceeding from the operator to the subject, prevailed.

Second, the period of thirty-five years during which the influence of Braid's experiments predominated, showing that other methods, and especially that by the fixed gaze, were efficient in producing the hypnotic sleep.

Third, the short period during which the influence of Charcot and the Paris school prevailed.

Fourth, the period since Bernheim began to publish his experiments, and which may be called the period of suggestion.

With this brief sketch in mind, we are prepared to examine some of the more important phenomena of hypnotism, both in its early and its later developments. A simple case would be as follows :—

A patient comes to the physician's office complaining of continual headaches, general debility, nervousness, and unsatisfactory sleep. She is willing to be hypnotized, and is accompanied by a friend. The physician seats her comfortably in a chair, and, seating himself opposite her, he takes her thumbs lightly between his own thumbs and fingers, asks her to look steadily at some convenient object—perhaps a shirt-stud or a specified button upon his coat. Presently her eyelids quiver and then droop slowly over her eyes; he gently closes them with the tips of his fingers, holds them lightly for a moment, and she is asleep.

He then makes several slow passes over her face and down the front of her body from head to foot, also some over her head and away from it, all without contact and without speaking to her. He lets her sleep ten or fifteen minutes—longer, if convenient—and then, making two or three upward passes over her face, he says promptly: "All right; wake up."

She slowly opens her eyes, probably smiles, and looks a little foolish at having slept. He inquires how she feels. She replies:

"I feel remarkably well—so rested—as though I had slept a whole night."

"How is your head?"

(Looking surprised.) "It is quite well—the pain is all gone."

"Very well," he says. "You will continue to feel better and stronger, and you will have good sleep at night."

And so it proves. Bernheim or a pupil of his would sit, or perhaps stand, near his patient, and in a quiet but firm voice talk of sleep.

"Sleep is what you need. Sleep is helpful and will do you good. Already, while I am talking to you, you are beginning to feel drowsy. Your eyes are tired; your lids are drooping; you are growing more and more sleepy; your lids droop more and more."

Then, if the eyelids seem heavy, he presses them down over the eyes, all the time affirming sleep. If sleep comes, he has succeeded; if not, he resorts to gestures, passes, the steady gaze, or whatever he thinks likely to aid his suggestion.

When the patient is asleep he suggests that when she awakes her pains and nervousness will be gone, and that she will have quiet and refreshing sleep at night. What is the condition of the patient while under the influence of this induced sleep? Pulse and respiration are little, if at all, changed; they may be slightly accelerated at first, and later, if very deep sleep occurs, they may be slightly retarded. Temperature is seldom changed at all, though, if abnormally high before the sleep is induced, it frequently falls during the sleep.

If the hand be raised, or the arm be drawn up high above the head, generally it will remain elevated until it is touched and replaced, or the patient is told that he can let it fall, when he slowly lowers it.

In many cases the limbs of the patient may be flexed or the body placed in any position, and that position will be retained for a longer or shorter period, sometimes for hours, without change. Sometimes the condition is one of rigidity so firm that the head may be placed upon one chair and the heels upon another, and the body will remain stiff like a bridge from one chair to the other, even when a heavy weight is placed upon the middle of the patient's body or another person is seated upon it. This is the full cataleptic condition.

Sometimes the whole body will be in a condition of anæsthesia, so that needles may be thrust deep into the flesh without evoking any sign of pain or any sensation whatever. Sometimes, when this condition of anæsthesia does not appear with the sleep, it may be induced by passes, or by suggesting that a certain limb or the whole body is without feeling. In this condition the most serious surgical operations have been performed without the slightest suffering on the part of the patient.

From the deep sleep the patient often passes

of his own accord into a condition in which he walks, talks, reads, writes, and obeys the slightest wish or suggestion of the hypnotizer—and yet he is asleep. This is called the alert stage, or the condition of somnambulism, and is the most peculiar, interesting, and wonderful of all.

The two chief stages of the hypnotic condition, then, are, first: the lethargic stage; second, the alert stage.

The stage of lethargy may be very light—a mere drowsiness—or very deep—a heavy slumber—and it is often accompanied by a cataleptic state, more or less marked in degree.

The alert stage may also vary and may be characterized by somnambulism, varying in character from a simple sleepy "yes" or "no" in answer to questions asked by his hypnotizer, to the most wonderful, even supranormal, mental activity.

From any of these states the subject may be awakened by his hypnotizer simply making a few upward passes or by saying in a firm voice, "All right, wake up," or, again, by affirming to the patient that he will awake when he (the hypnotizer) has counted up to a certain number, as, for instance, five.

Generally, upon awakening, the subject has no

knowledge or remembrance of anything which has transpired during his hypnotic condition. This is known as amnesia. Sometimes, however, a hazy recollection of what has happened remains, especially if the hypnotic condition has been only slight.

Up to the present time hypnotism has been studied from two separate and important standpoints and for two well-defined purposes: (1) For its therapeutic effects, or its use in the treatment of disease and relief of pain; (2) for the mental or psychical phenomena which it presents.

The following cases will illustrate its study and use from the therapeutic standpoint—and, first, two cases treated by the old mesmerists, 1843–53. They are from reports published in The Zoist:—

(1) Q. I. P., a well-known artist, fifty years ago, had been greatly troubled and distressed by weak and inflamed eyes, accompanied by ulceration of the cornea, a condition which had lasted more than four years. He was never free from the disease, and often it was so severe as to prevent work in his studio, and especially reading, for months at a time. He had been under the care of the best oculists, both in New York and London, for long periods and at different times, but

with very little temporary and no permanent relief.

He was urged, as a last resort, to try animal magnetism, as it was then called. Accordingly, he consulted a mesmeric practitioner in London, and was treated by passes made over the back of the head and down the spine and from the centre of the forehead backward and outward over the temples and down the sides of the head.

All other treatment was discontinued. No mesmeric phenomena of any kind were produced, not even sleep, but from the first day a degree of comfort and also improvement was experienced.

The treatment was given one hour daily for one month. The improvement was decided and uninterrupted, such as had never before been experienced under any form of medical or surgical treatment, no matter how thoroughly carried out. The general health was greatly improved, and the eyes were so much benefited that they could be relied upon constantly, both for painting and reading, and the cure was permanent.

(2) A case of rheumatism treated by Dr. Elliotson of London. The patient, G. F., age thirty-five years, was a laborer, and had suffered from rheumatism seven weeks. When he applied to Dr. Elliotson, the doctor was sitting in his office,

in company with three friends—one a medical gentleman, and all skeptics regarding mesmerism.

They all, however, expressed a desire to see the treatment, and, accordingly, the patient was brought in. He came with difficulty, upon crutches, his face betokening extreme pain. He had never been mesmerized.

The doctor sat down opposite his patient, took his thumbs in his hands, and gazed steadily in his eyes. In twenty minutes he fell into the mesmeric sleep. Several of the mesmeric phenomena were then produced in the presence of his skeptical friends, after which he was allowed to sleep undisturbed for two hours. No suggestions regarding his disease are reported as having been made to the patient during his sleep.

He was awakened by reverse passes. Being fairly aroused, he arose from his chair, walked up and down the room without difficulty, and was perfectly unconscious of all that had transpired during his sleep; he only knew he came into the room suffering, and on crutches, and that he was now free from pain and could walk with ease without them. He left one crutch with the doctor and went out twirling the other in his hand. He remained perfectly well.

Dr. Elliotson afterward tried on three different

occasions to hypnotize him but without success. Others also tried, but all attempts in this direction failed.

I will here introduce one or two cases from my own notebook:—

(1) A. C., a young girl of Irish parentage, fifteen years old, light skin, dark hair and eyes, and heavy eyebrows. Her father had "fits" for several years previous to his death. I first saw the patient Dec. 4, 1872; this was five years before Charcot's experiments, and nearly ten years before those of Bernheim.

She was then having frequent epileptic attacks, characterized by sudden loss of consciousness, convulsions, foaming at the mouth, biting the tongue, and dark color. She had her first attack six months before I saw her, and they had increased in frequency and in severity until now they occurred twenty or more times a day, sometimes lasting many minutes, and sometimes only a few seconds; sometimes they were of very great severity.

She had received many falls, burns, and bruises in consequence of their sudden accession. They occurred both day and night. On my second visit I determined to try hypnotism. Patient went to sleep in eight minutes, slept a short time and awoke without interference. She was immediately put to sleep again; she slept only a few minutes, and again awoke.

Dec. 7.—Her friends report that the attacks have not been so frequent and not nearly so violent since my last visit. Hypnotized; patient went into a profound sleep and remained one hour; she was then awakened by reverse passes.

Dec. 8.—The attacks have been still less frequent and severe; she has slept quietly; appetite good. Hypnotized and allowed her to sleep two hours, and then awoke her by the upward passes.

Dec. 9.—There has been still more marked improvement; the attacks have been very few, none lasting more than half a minute. Hypnotized and allowed her to remain asleep three hours. Awoke her with some difficulty, and she was still somewhat drowsy when I left. She went to sleep in the afternoon and slept soundly four hours; awoke and ate her supper; went to sleep again and slept soundly all night.

Dec. 10.—There has been no return of the attacks. A month later she had had no return of the attacks. She soon after left town, and I have not heard of her since. In this case no suggestions whatever were made.

(2) B. X., twenty-four years of age, a sporting

man; obstinate, independent, self-willed, a leader in his circle. He had been a hard drinker from boyhood. He had been injured by a fall three years before, and had been subject to severe attacks of hæmatemesis. I had known him for three or four months previous to June, 1891. At that time he came into my office one evening somewhat under the influence of alcoholic stimulants. After talking a few moments, I advised him to lie down on the lounge. I made no remarks about his drinking, nor about sleep. I simply took his two thumbs in my hands and sat quietly beside him. Presently I made a few long passes from head to feet, and in five minutes he was fast asleep.

His hands and arms, outstretched and raised high up, remained exactly as they were placed. Severe pinching elicited no sign of sensation. He was in the deep hypnotic sleep.

I then spoke to him in a distinct and decided manner. I told him he was ruining his life and making his family very unhappy by his habit of intemperance. I then told him very decidedly that when he awoke he would have no more desire for alcoholic stimulants of any kind; that he would look upon them all as his enemies, and he would refuse them under all circumstances; that even the smell of them would be disagreeable to him. I repeated the suggestions and then awoke him by making a few passes upward over his face, I did not inform him that I had hypnotized him, nor speak to him at all about his habit of drinking. I prescribed for some ailment for which he had visited me and he went away.

I neither saw nor heard from him again for three months, when I received a letter from him from a distant city, informing me that he had not drank a drop of spirituous liquor since he was in my office that night. His health was perfect, and he had no more vomiting of blood.

June, 1892, one year from the time I had hypnotized him, he came into my office in splendid condition. He had drank nothing during the whole year. I have not heard from him since.

The following case illustrates Bernheim's method:—

Mlle. J., teacher, thirty-two years old, came to the clinique, Feb. 17, 1887, for chorea, or St. Vitus's dance. Nearly two weeks previous she had been roughly reprimanded by her superior which had greatly affected her. She could scarcely sleep or eat; she had nausea, pricking sensations in both arms, delirium at times, and now incessant movements, sometimes as frequent as two every second, in both the right arm and leg.

She can neither write nor attend to her school duties. Bernheim hypnotizes her by his method. She goes easily into the somnambulic condition. In three or four minutes, under the influence of suggestion, the movements of the hand and foot cease; upon waking up, they reappear, but less frequently. A second hypnotization, with suggestion, checks them completely.

FEB. 19th.—Says she has been very comfortable; the pricking sensations have ceased. No nervous movements until nine o'clock this morning, when they returned, about ten or eleven every minute. New hypnotization and suggestion, during which the motions cease, and they remain absent when she wakes.

21st.—Has had slight pains and a few choraic movements.

25th.—Is doing well; has no movements; says she is cured.

She returned a few times during the next four months with slight nervous movements, which were promptly relieved by hypnotizing and suggestion.

Bernheim, in his book, "Suggestive Therapeutics," gives details of over one hundred cases, mostly neuralgic and rheumatic, most of which are described as cured, either quickly or by repeated hypnotization and suggestion.

The Zoist, a journal devoted to psychology and mesmerism nearly fifty years ago, gives several hundred cases of treatment and cure by the early mesmerists, some of them very remarkable, and also many cases of surgical operations of the most severe or dangerous character painlessly done under the anæsthetic influence of mesmerism before the benign effects of ether or chloroform were known. These cases are not often referred to by the modern student of hypnotism. Nevertheless, they constitute a storehouse of well-observed facts which have an immense interest and value.

It will thus be seen that throughout the whole history of hypnotism, under whatever name it has been studied, one of its chief features has been its power to relieve suffering and cure disease; and at the present day, while many physicians who are quite ignorant of its uses, in general terms deny its practicability, few who have any real knowledge of it are so unjust or regardless of facts as to deny its therapeutic effects.

CHAPTER III.

HYPNOTISM—PSYCHICAL ASPECT.

As before remarked the phenomena of hypnotism may be viewed from two distinct standpoints —one, that from which the physical and especially the therapeutic features are most prominent, the standpoint from which we have already viewed the subject; the other is the psychical or mental aspect, which presents phenomena no less striking, and is the one which is especially attractive to the most earnest students of psychology.

The hypnotic condition has been variously divided and subdivided by different students and different writers upon the subject; Charicot, for instance, makes three distinct states, which he designates (1) catalepsy, (2) lethargy, and (3) somnambulism, while Bernheim proposes five states, or, as he designates them, degrees of hypnotism, namely, (1) sleepiness, (2) light sleep, (3) deep sleep, (4) very deep sleep, (5) somnambulism.

All these divisions are arbitrary and unnatural;

Bernheim's five degrees have no definite limit or line of separation one from the other, and Charcot's condition of catalepsy is only lethargy or sleep in which the subject may, to a greater or less degree, maintain the position in which he is placed by his hypnotizer.

There are, however, as already stated, two distinct and definite conditions, namely, (1) lethargy, or the inactive stage, and (2) somnambulism, or the alert stage, and if, in examining the subject, we make this simple division, we shall free it from much confusion and unnecessary verbiage.

When a subject is hypnotized by any soothing process, he first experiences a sensation of drowsiness, and then in a space of time, usually varying from two to twenty minutes, he falls into a more or less profound slumber. His breathing is full and quiet, his pulse normal; he is unconscious of his surroundings; or possibly he may be quiet, restful, indisposed to move, but having a consciousness, probably dim and imperfect, of what is going on about him.

This is the condition of lethargy, and in it most subjects, but not all, retain to a greater or less degree whatever position the hypnotizer imposes upon them; they sleep on, often maintaining what, under ordinary circumstances, would be a most uncomfortable position, for hours, motionless as a statue of bronze or stone.

If, now, he speaks of his own accord, or his magnetizer speaks to him and he replies, he is in the somnambulic or alert stage. He may open his eyes, talk in a clear and animated manner; he may walk about, and show even more intellectual acuteness and physical activity than when in his normal state, or he may merely nod assent or answer slowly to his hypnotizer's questions; still, he is in the somnambulic or alert stage of hypnotism.

The following are some of the phenomena which have been observed in this stage. It is not necessary to rehearse the stock performances of lecture-room hypnotists. While under the influence of hypnotic suggestion a lad, for instance, is made to go through the pantomime of fishing in an imaginary brook, a dignified man to canter around the stage on all fours, under the impression that he is a pony, or watch an imaginary mouse-hole in the most alert and interested manner while believing himself a cat; or the subject is made to take castor oil with every expression of delight, or reject the choicest wines with disgust, believing them to be nauseous drugs, or stagger with drunkenness under the influence of a glass of pure water, supposed to be whisky.

All these things have been done over and over for the last forty years, and people have not known whether to consider them a species of necromancy or well-practiced tricks, in which the performers were accomplices, or, perhaps, a few more thoughtful and better-instructed people have looked upon them as involving psychological problems of the greatest interest, which might some day strongly influence all our systems of mental philosophy.

But whether done by the mesmerist of forty years ago or the hypnotist of the past decade, they were identical in character, and were simply genuine examples of the great power of suggestion when applied to persons under the mesmeric or hypnotic influence. Such exhibitions, however, are unnecessary and undignified, if not positively degrading, to both subject and operator, whether given by the self-styled professor of the town-hall platform or the aspiring clinical professor of nervous diseases before his packed amphitheatre of admiring students.

One of the most singular as well as important points in connection with hypnotism is the rapport or relationship which exists between the hypnotizer and the hypnotized subject. The manner in which the hypnotic sleep is induced is of little importance. The important thing, if results of any kind are to be obtained, is that rapport should be established.

This relationship is exhibited in various ways. Generally, while in the hypnotic state, the subject hears no voice but that of his hypnotizer; he does no bidding but his, he receives no suggestions but from him, and no one else can awaken him from his sleep.

If another person interferes, trying to impose his influence upon the sleeping subject, or attempts to waken him, distressing and even alarming results may appear. The degree to which this rapport exists varies greatly in different cases, but almost always, perhaps we should say always, the condition exists in some degree. In some rare cases this rapport is of a still higher and more startling character, exhibiting phenomena so contrary to, or rather, so far exceeding, our usual experience as to be a surprise to all and a puzzle to the wisest.

One of these curious phenomena is well exhibited in what is known as community of sensation, or the perception by the subject of sensations experienced by the operator. The following experiment, observed by Mr. Gurney and Dr. Myers of the Society for Psychical Research, will illustrate this phase of the subject.

The sensitive in this experiment is designated as Mr. C., and the operator as Mr. S. There was no contact or any communication whatsoever of the ordinary kind between them. C. was hypnotized, but was not informed of the nature of the experiment which was to be tried. The operator stood behind the hypnotized subject, and Mr. Gurney, standing behind the operator, handed him the different substances to be used in the experiment, and he, in turn, placed them in his own mouth.

Salt was first so tasted by the operator, whereupon the subject, C., instantly and loudly cried out: "What's that salt stuff?" Sugar was given. C. replied, "Sweeter; not so bad as before." Powdered ginger; reply, "Hot, dries up your mouth; reminds me of mustard." Sugar given again; reply, "A little better—a sweetish taste." Other substances were tried, with similar results, the last one tasted being vinegar, when it was found that C. had fallen into the deeper lethargic condition and made no reply.

Another experiment is reported by Dr. William A. Hammond of Washington. The doctor said:

"A most remarkable fact is, that some few subjects of hypnotism experience sensations from impressions made upon the hypnotizer. Thus, there is a subject upon whom I sometimes operate whom I can shut up in a room with an observer, while I go into another closed room at a distance of one hundred feet or more with another observer. This one, for instance, scratches my hand with a pin, and instantly the hypnotized subject rubs his corresponding hand, and says, 'Don't scratch my hand so;' or my hair is pulled, and immediately he puts his hand to his head and says, 'Don't pull my hair;' and so on, feeling every sensation that I experience."

This experiment, it must be borne in mind, is conducted in closed rooms a hundred feet apart, and through at least two partitions or closed doors, and over that distance and through these intervening obstacles peculiar and definite sensations experienced by one person are perceived and definitely described by another person, no ordinary means of communication existing between them. This is an example of the rapport existing between the operator and hypnotized subject carried to an unusual degree.

The following experiments are examples of hypnotizing at a distance, or telepathic hypnotism, and while illustrating still further the rapport, or curious relationship, existing between hypnotizer and subject, are also illustrations of the rarer psychic phenomena of hypnotism.

The first series of experiments is given by Prof. Pierre Janet of Havre and Dr. Gibert, a prominent physician of the same city. The subject was Mme. B., a heavy, rather stolid, middle-aged peasant woman, without any ambition for notoriety, or to be known as a sensitive; on the contrary, she disliked it, and the experiments were disagreeable to her. She was, however an excellent example of close rapport with her hypnotizer.

While in the deep sleep, and perfectly insensible to ordinary stimuli, however violent, contact, or even the proximity of her hypnotizer's hand, caused contractures, which a light touch from him would also remove. No one else could produce the slightest effect. After about ten minutes in this deep trance she usually passed into the alert, or somnambulic stage, from which also no one but the operator could arouse her. Hypnotization was difficult or impossible unless the operator concentrated his thoughts upon the desired result, but by simply willing, without passes or any physical means whatsoever, the hypnotic condition could be quickly induced.

Various experiments in simply willing post-hypnotic acts, without suggestion through any of the ordinary channels of communication, were also perfectly successful. Dr. Gibert then made three experiments in putting this subject to sleep when she was in another part of the town, a third of a mile away from the operator, and at a time fixed by a third person, the experiment also being wholly unexpected by the subject.

On two of these occasions Prof. Janet found the subject in a deep trance ten minutes after the willing to sleep, and no one but Dr. Gibert, who had put her to sleep, could rouse her. In the third experiment the subject experienced the hypnotic influence and desire to sleep, but resisted it and kept herself awake by washing her hands in cold water.

During a second series of experiments made with the same subject, several members of the Society for Psychical Research were present and took an active part in them. Apart from trials made in the same or an adjoining room, twenty-one experiments were made when the subject was at distances varying from one-half to three-fourths of a mile away from her hypnotizer. Of these, six were reckoned as failures, or only partial successes; there remained, then, fifteen perfect successes in which the subject, Mme. B., was found entranced fifteen minutes after the willing or mental suggestion. During one of these experiments, the subject was willed by Dr. Gibert to come through several intervening streets to him at his own house, which she accomplished in the somnambulic condition, and under the observation of Prof. Janet and several other physicians.

Another series of experiments was made with another subject by Dr. Héricourt, one of Prof. Richet's coadjutors. The experiments included the gradual extension of the distance through which the willing power was successful, first to another room, then to another street, and a distant part of the city.

One day, while attempting to hypnotize her in another street, three hundred yards distant, at 3 o'clock P. M., he was suddenly called away to attend a patient, and forgot all about his hypnotic subject. Afterward he remembered that he was to meet her at 4:30, and went to keep his appointment. But not finding her, he thought possibly the experiment, which had been interrupted might, after all, have proved successful. Upon this supposition, at 5 o'clock he willed her to awake.

That evening, without being questioned at all, she gave the following account of herself: At

3 P. M. she was overcome by an irresistible desire to sleep, a most unusual thing for her at that hour. She went into an adjoining room, fell insensible upon a sofa, where she was afterward found by her servant, cold and motionless, as if dead.

Attempts on the part of the servant to rouse her proved ineffectual, but gave her great distress. She woke spontaneously and free from pain at 5 o'clock.

By no means the least interesting of the higher phenomena of hypnotism are post-hypnotic suggestions, or the fulfilment after waking of suggestions impressed upon the subject when asleep.

A few summers ago at a little gathering of intelligent people, much interest was manifested and a general desire to see some hypnotic experiments. Accordingly, one of the ladies whose good sense and good faith could not be doubted, was hypnotized and put into the condition of profound lethargy. After a few slight experiments, exhibiting anæsthesia, hallucinations of taste, plastic pose, and the like, I said to her in a decided manner :

"Now I am about to waken you. I will count five, and when I say the word 'five' you will promptly, but quietly and without any excitement, awake. Your mind will be perfectly clear, and you will feel rested and refreshed by your sleep. Presently you will approach Mrs. O., and will be attracted by the beautiful shell comb which she wears in her hair, and you will ask her to permit you to examine it."

I then commenced counting slowly, and at the word "five" she awoke, opened her eyes promptly, looked bright and happy, and expressed herself as feeling comfortable and greatly rested, as though she had slept through a whole night. She rose from her chair, mingled with the company, and presently approaching Mrs. O., exclaimed:

"What a beautiful comb! Please allow me to examine it."

And suiting the action to the word, she placed her hand lightly on the lady's head, examined the comb, and expressed great admiration for it; in short, she fulfilled with great exactness the whole suggestion.

She was perfectly unconscious that any suggestion had been made to her; she was greatly surprised to see that she was the centre of observation, and especially at the ripple of laughter which greeted her admiration of the comb.

To another young lady, hypnotized in like manner, I suggested that on awaking she should approach the young daughter of our hostess, who was present, holding a favorite kitten in her arms, and should say to her, "What a pretty kitten you have! What is her name?"

The suggestion was fulfilled to the letter. It was only afterward that I learned that this young lady had a very decided aversion to cats, and always avoided them if possible.

Suggestions for post-hypnotic fulfilment are sometimes carried out after a considerable time has elapsed, and upon the precise day suggested.

Bernheim, in August, 1883, suggested to S., an old soldier, while in the hypnotic sleep, that upon the 3d of October following, sixty-three days after the suggestion, he should go to Dr. Liébeault's house; that he would there see the President of the Republic, who would give to him a medal.

Promptly on the day designated he went. Dr. Liébeault states that S. came at 12:50 o'clock; he greeted M. F., who met him at the door as he came in, and then went to the left side of the office without paying any attention to any one. Dr. Lièbeault continues:—

"I saw him bow respectfully and heard him speak the word 'Excellence.' Just then he held out his right hand, and said, 'Thank your Excellence.' Then I asked him to whom he was speaking. 'Why, to the President of the Republic.' He then bowed, and a few minutes later took his departure."

A patient of my own, a young man with whom I occasionally experiment, exhibits some of the different phases and phenomena of hypnotism in a remarkable manner. He goes quickly into the stage of profound lethargy; after allowing him to sleep a few moments, I say to him: "Now you can open your eyes and you can see and talk with me, but you are still asleep, and you will remember nothing."

He opens his eyes at once, smiles, gets up and walks, and chats in a lively manner. If I say: "Now you are in the deep sleep again," and pass my hand downward before his eyes, immediately his eyes close and he is in a profound slumber. If five seconds later I again say, "Now you can open your eyes," he is again immediately in the alert stage.

For experiment I then take half a dozen plain blank cards, exactly alike, and in one corner of one of the cards I put a minute dot, so that upon close inspection it can be recognized. Holding these in my hand, I say to him:

"Here are six cards; five of them are blank, but this one (the one I have marked, he only seeing the plain side) has a picture of myself upon it. It is a particularly good picture, and I have had it prepared specially for this occasion. Do you see the picture?"

"Of course I do," he replies. "What do you think of it?" I ask him. He looks at me carefully and compares my face with the suggested picture on the card and replies, "It is excellent."

"Very well, give me the cards."

He hands them to me and I shuffle and disarrange them as much as possible. I then show them to him, holding them in my hand, and say:

"Now show me the card which has my picture upon it."

He selects it at once. I only know it is correct by looking for the dot upon the back, which has all the while been kept carefully concealed from him.

I then say to him: "Now, I am going to awaken you, and when awake you will come to the desk, select from the cards which I now place there the one which has my picture, and show it to me."

He awakes at my counting when I reach the word five, as I have suggested to him. He remembers nothing of what has passed since he was hypnotized, but thinks he has had a long and delightful sleep. I sit at my desk; he walks up to it, examines the six cards which are lying there, selects one, and showing it to me, remarks, "There is your picture." It was the same marked card.

On another occasion, while he was asleep and in the alert stage, Mrs. M. was present. I introduced her, and he spoke to her with perfect propriety. Afterward I said: "Now, I will awake you, but you will only see me. Mrs. M. you will not see at all."

I then awoke him, as usual. He commenced talking to me in a perfectly natural and unrestrained manner. Mrs. M. stood by my side between him and myself, but he paid not the slightest attention to her; she then withdrew, and I remarked indifferently:

"Wasn't it a little peculiar of you not to speak to Mrs. M. before she went out?"

"Speak to Mrs. M!" he exclaimed, with evident surprise. "I did not know she had been in the room."

One day when Drs. Liébeault and Bernheim were together at their clinic at the hospital, Dr. Liébeault suggested to a hypnotized patient that when she awoke she would no longer see Dr. Bernheim, but that she would recognize his hat, would put it on her head, and offer to take it to him.

When she awoke, Dr. Bernheim was standing in front of her. She was asked: "Where is Dr. Bernheim?" She replied: "He is gone, but here is his hat."

Dr. Bernheim then said to her, "Here I am, madam; I am not gone, you recognize me, perfectly."

She was silent, taking not the slightest notice of him. Some one else addressed her; she replied with perfect propriety. Finally, when about to go out she took up Dr. Bernheim's hat, put it on her head, saying she would take it to him; but to her Dr. Bernheim was not present.

To the number of curious phenomena, both physical and mental, connected with hypnotism, it is difficult to find a limit; a few others seem too important in their bearing upon the subject to be omitted, even in this hasty survey.

Some curious experiments in the production of local anæsthesia were observed by the committee on mesmerism from the Society for Psychical Research.

The subject was in his normal condition and blindfolded; his arms were then passed through holes in a thick paper screen, extending in front of him and far above his head, and his ten fingers were spread out upon a table. Two of the fingers were then silently pointed out by a third person to Mr. S., the operator, who proceeded to make passes over the designated fingers.

Care was taken that such a distance was maintained between the fingers of the subject and operator that no contact was possible, and no currents of air or sensation of heat were produced by which the subject might possibly divine which of his fingers were the subject of experiment. In short, the strictest test conditions in every particular, were observed. After the passes had been continued for a minute, or even less time, the operator simply holding his own fingers pointed downward toward the designated fingers of the subject, the two fingers so treated were found to be perfectly stiff and insensible. A strong current of electricity, wounding with a pointed instrument, burning with a match—all failed to elicit the slightest sign of pain or discomfort, while the slightest injury to the unmagnetized fingers quickly elicited cries and protests. When told to double up his fist the two magnetized fingers remained rigid and immovable, and utterly refused to be folded up with the others.

A series of one hundred and sixty experiments of this character was made with five different subjects. Of these, only seven were failures. In another series of forty-one experiments this curious fact was observed. In all these experiments the operator, while making the passes in the same manner and under the same conditions as in the former series, silently willed that the effect should not follow; that is, that insensibility and rigidity should not occur. In thirty-six of these experiments insensibility did not occur; in five cases the insensibility and rigidity occurred—in two cases perfectly, in three imperfectly.

That some quality is imparted even to inanimate objects by some mesmerizers, by passes or handling, through which a sensitive or subject is able to recognize and select that object from among many others, seems to be a well-established fact. The following experiments are in point:—

A gentleman well known to the committee of investigation, and who was equally interested with it in securing reliable results, was selected as a subject. He was accustomed to be hypnotized by the operator, but in the present case he remained perfectly in his normal condition.

One member of the committee took the subject

into a separate room on another floor and engaged him closely in conversation. The operator remained with other members of the committee. Ten small miscellaneous articles, such as a piece of sealing wax, a penknife, paperweight, card-case, pocketbook, and similar articles were scattered upon a table. One was designated by the committee, over which the mesmerist made passes, sometimes with light contact.

This was continued for one or two minutes, and when the process was completed the mesmerist was conducted out and to a third room. The articles were then rearranged in a manner quite different from that in which they had been left by the operator, and the subject from the floor above was brought into the room. The several objects were then examined by the sensitive, who upon taking the mesmerized object in his hand, immediately recognized it as the one treated by his mesmerizer.

The experiment was then varied by using ten small volumes exactly alike. One volume was selected by the committee, over which the operator simply made passes with out any contact whatsoever. Three or four other volumes of the set were also handled and passes made over them by a member of the committee.

MAGNETIZED WATER DETECTED.

The operator then being excluded, the sensitive was brought in and immediately selected the magnetized volume. This he did four times in succession. In reply to the question as to how he was able to distinguish the magnetized object from others, he said that when he took the right object in his hand he experienced a mild tingling sensation.

My own experiments with magnetized water have presented similar results. The water was treated by simply holding the fingers of both hands brought together in a clump, for about a minute just over the cup of water, but without any contact whatsoever. This water was then given to the subject without her knowing that she was taking part in an experiment; but alternating it or giving it irregularly with water which had not been so treated, and given by a third person, in every case the magnetized water was at once detected with great certainty. In describing the sensation produced by the magnetized water one patient said the sensation was an agreeable warmth and stimulation upon the tongue, another that it was a "sparkle" like aerated water; it sparkled in her mouth and all the way down into her stomach. Such are a few among the multitude of facts and phenomena relating to hypnotism. They suffice to settle and make sure some matters which until lately have been looked upon as questionable, and, on the other hand, they bring into prominence others of the greatest interest which demand further study.

Among the subjects which may be considered established may be placed,

(1) The reality of the hypnotic condition.

(2) The increased and unusual power of suggestion over the hypnotized subject.

(3) The usefulness of hypnotism as a therapeutic agent.

(4) The perfect reality and natural, as contrasted with supernatural, character of many wonderful phenomena, both physical and psychical, exhibited in the hypnotic state.

On the other hand, much remains for future study;

(1) The exact nature of the influence which produces the hypnotic condition is not known.

(2) Neither is the nature of the rapport or peculiar relationship which exists between the hypnotizer and the hypnotized subject—a relationship which is sometimes so close that the subject hears no voice but that of his hypnotizer, perceives and experiences the same sensations of taste,

touch, and feeling generally as are experienced by him, and can be awakened only by him.

(3) Nor is it known by what peculiar process suggestion is rendered so potent, turning, for the time being, at least, water into wine, vulgar weeds into choicest flowers, a lady's drawing-room into a fishpond, and clear skies and quiet waters into lightning-rent storm-clouds and tempest-tossed waves; turning laughter into sadness, and tears into mirth.

In dealing with the subject of hypnotism in this hasty and general way, only such facts and phenomena have been presented as are well known and accepted by well-informed students of the subjects. Others still more wonderful will later claim our attention.

CHAPTER IV.

LUCIDITY OR CLAIRVOYANCE.

WHILE there is doubtess a recognized standard of normal perception, yet the acuteness with which sensations are perceived by different individuals, even in ordinary health, passes through a wide scale of variation, both above and below this standard. The difference in the ability to see and recognize natural objects, signs, and indications, between the ordinary city denizen and, for instance, the American Indian or the white frontiersman, hunter, or scout, is something marvellous.

So, also, regarding the power to distinguish colors. One person may not be able to distinguish even the simple or primary colors, as, for example, red from blue or green, while the weavers of Central or Eastern Asia distinguish with certainty two hundred or three hundred shades which are entirely undistinguishable to ordinary Western eyes.

So of sound. One ear can hardly be said to make any distinction whatever regarding pitch, while to another the slightest variation is perfectly perceptible. Some even do not hear at all sounds above or below a certain pitch; some persons of ordinary hearing within a certain range of pitch, nevertheless, have never heard the song of the canary bird, and perhaps have lived through a large portion of their lives without even knowing that it was a song-bird at all. Its song was above the range of their hearing. Some never hear the sound of the piccolo, or octave flute, while others miss entirely the lowest notes of the organ.

There is the same great difference in perception by touch, taste, and smell. In certain conditions of disease, accompanied by great depression of the vital forces, this deviation from normal perception is greatly increased. I have had a patient who presented the following briefly-outlined phenomena:—

After a long illness, during which other interesting psychical phenomena were manifested, as convalescence progressed, I had occasion to notice instances of supernormal perception, and to test it I made use of the following expedient: Taking an old-fashioned copper cent, I carefully enveloped it in a piece of ordinary tissue paper. This was then covered by another and then another, until the coin had acquired six complete envelopes of the paper, and formed a little flat parcel, easily held in the palm of my hand.

Taking this with me, I visited my patient. She was lying upon a sofa, and as I entered the room I took a chair and sat leisurely down beside her, having the little package close in the palm of my right hand. I took her right hand in mine in such a manner that the little package was between our hands in close contact with her palm as well as my own. I remarked upon the weather and commenced the routine duty of feeling her pulse with my left hand. A minute or two was then passed in banter and conversation, designed to thoroughly engage her attention, when all at once she commenced to wipe her mouth with her handkerchief and to spit and sputter with her tongue and lips, as if to rid herself of some offensive taste or substance. She then looked up suspiciously at me and said:

"I wonder what you are doing with me now."

Then suddenly pulling her hand away from mine she exclaimed:

"I know what it is; you have put a nasty piece of copper in my hand."

Through all these coverings the coppery emanation from the coin had penetrated her system, reached her tongue, and was perceptible to her supernormal taste.

This patient could distinguish with absolute certainty "mesmerized" water from that which had not been so treated; my finger, also, pointed at her even at a distance and when her back was turned to me caused convulsive action, and the same result followed when the experiment was made through a closed door, and when she did not suspect that I was in the neighborhood.

It will be seen, then, how marvellously the action of certain senses may be exalted by long and careful training on the one hand, and suddenly by disease on the other. We have seen, moreover, how some persons known as sensitives are able to receive impressions by thought-transference so as to name cards, repeat words and fictitious names, both of persons and places, merely thought of but not spoken by another person known as as the agent or operator, and to draw diagrams unmistakably like those formed in the mind or intently looked upon by the agent.

We have also seen how the hypnotized or mesmerized subject is able to detect objects which have only been touched or handled by the mesmerizer, and even to feel pain inflicted upon him, and recognize by taste substances put in the mesmerizer's mouth.

It will be seen, then, that not only increased but entirely supernormal perception on the part of some individuals is a well-established fact. But all these conditions of increased power of perception, and especially thought-transference, must be carefully distinguished from independent clairvoyance. It is not the purpose of this paper to discuss the method or philosophy of clairvoyance, but simply to call attention to well-authenticated facts illustrating the exercise of this power, and to briefly point to the current theories regarding it.

A belief in supernormal perception, and especially in the clairvoyant vision, is apparent in the history, however meagre it may be, of every ancient nation.

Hebrew history is full of instances of it. A striking example is recorded as occurring during the long war between Syria and Israel. The King of Syria had good reasons for suspecting that in some manner the King of Israel was made acquainted with all his intended military operations, since he was always prepared to thwart them at every point. Accordingly he called together his chiefs and demanded to know who it was among them who thus favored the King of Israel, to which one of the chiefs replied: "It is none of thy servants, O King: but Elisha, a prophet that is in Israel, telleth the King of Israel the words that thou speakest in thy chamber."

Pythagoras, a century before the time of Socrates, found this faculty believed in, and made use of in Egypt, Babylon, and India, and he himself, as the founder of the early Greek philosophy and culture, practised and taught the esoteric as well as the exoteric methods of acquiring knowledge, and he is credited with having acquired by esoteric methods—internal or mental perception and clairvoyant vision—a knowledge of the true theory of the solar system as expounded and demonstrated in a later day by Copernicus.

As an example of responses by the Greek oracles, take the experience of Crœsus, the rich King of Lydia. He sent messengers to ascertain if the Pythoness could tell what he, the King of Lydia, was doing on a certain specified day. The answer came:—

> "I number the sands—I fathom the sea.
> I hear the dumb—I know the thoughts of the silent.
> There cometh to me the odor of lamb's flesh.
> It is seething, mixed with the flesh of a tortoise.
> Brass is beneath it, and brass is also above it."

The messenger returned and delivered the reply,

when he found that Crœsus, in order to do something most unlikely to be either guessed or discovered, had cut in pieces a lamb and a tortoise, and seethed them together in a brazen vessel having a brazen cover.

Apollonius Tyaneus, a Pythagorian philosopher and chief of a school of philosophy which was the predecessor of the Alexandrian Neo-Platonists, is credited with most remarkable clairvoyant powers. Many instances of this faculty are recorded and believed upon the best of ancient authority.

One instance relates to the assassination of Domitian. Apollonius was in the midst of a discourse at Ephesus, when suddenly he stopped as though having lost his train of thought. After a moment's hesitation, to the astonishment of his auditors, he cried out : "Strike! strike the tyrant." Seeing the surprise of the people he explained that at the very moment at which he had stopped in his discourse the tyrant was slain. Subsequent information proved that Domitian, the reigning tyrant, was assassinated at that very moment.

Ancient historians, philosophers and poets all unite in defending the truth of the oracles and their power of perceiving events transpiring at a distance, and also of foreseeing those in the future. Herodotus gives more than seventy examples of oracular responses, dreams and portents which he affirms were literally fulfilled. Livy gives more than fifty, Cicero many striking cases ; and Xenophon, Plato, Tacitus, Suetonius, and a host of other writers all give evidence in the same direction. Now whether these responses and visions were, as all these intelligent people supposed, from a supernatural source, or as we shall endeavor to show, had their origin in certain faculties naturally appertaining to the mind, and which at certain times and under certain favorable circumstances came into activity, it certainly shows that the most intelligent men amongst all the most cultivated nations of the past have been firm believers in the reality of clairvoyance.

Coming down to later times, Emanuel Swedenborg, and Frederica Hauffé, the seeress of Proverst, were marked examples of the clairvoyant faculty. Some have affected to discredit Swedenborg's clairvoyant powers, but apart from his revelations regarding a spiritual world, which, of course, it is at present impossible to substantiate, whatever may be our belief regarding them, if human testimony is to be regarded of any value whatever in matters of this kind, the following oft-told incident should be counted as established for a verity.

On a Saturday afternoon in September, 1756, Swedenborg arrived in Gottenburg from England. Gottenburg is three hundred miles from Stockholm, which was the home of Swedenborg. On the same evening he was the guest of Mr. William Castel, with fifteen other persons, who were invited to meet him, and who, on that account, may be supposed to have been of more than ordinary consequence and intelligence.

About six o'clock Swedenborg seemed preoccupied and restless. He went out into the street, but soon returned, anxious and disturbed. He said that at that moment a great fire was raging at Stockholm. He declared that the house of one of his friends was already destroyed, and that his own was in danger. At eight o'clock he announced that the fire was arrested only three doors from his own house.

The information, and the peculiar manner in which it was imparted, created a great sensation, not only in the company assembled at Mr. Castel's, but throughout the city. On Sunday morning the governor sent for Swedenborg, who gave him a detailed account of the conflagration and the course it had pursued. On Monday, the third day, a courier arrived from Stockholm, who also gave the governor a detailed account of the fire, which agreed in every respect with that already given by Swedenborg.

Nearly a century after Swedenborg, lived Mme. Hauffé, known as the seeress of Proverst. She died in 1829 at the age of twenty-eight years. As a child she exhibited peculiar psychical tendencies, but it was only during the last six years of her life, and after exhausting illnesses, that her peculiar clairvoyant powers were conspicuously developed.

Justinus Kerner, an eminent physician and man of letters, was her attending physician during the last three years of her life, and afterward became her biographer. She first came under his care at Weinsberg in 1826. At that time her debility was excessive, and nearly every day she fell spontaneously into the somnambulic condition, became clairvoyant, and related her visions. On the day of her arrival at Weinsberg, having gone into this trance condition, she sent for Kerner but he refused to see her until she awoke. He then told her that he would never see her nor listen to her while she was in this abnormal state. I mention this simply to show that her physician was not then at all in sympathy with her regarding her peculiar psychological condition, though afterward he became thoroughly convinced of its genuineness and of her honesty. He relates the following incident, which, with many others, came under his own observation :—

Soon after her arrival at Weinsberg, and while still a perfect stranger to her surroundings, while in her somnambulic condition, she said that a man was near her and desired to speak with her, but that she could not understand what he wanted to say. She said he squinted terribly, and that his presence disturbed her, and she desired him to go away. On his second appearance, some weeks later, she said he brought with him a sheet of paper with figures upon it, and that he came up from a vault directly underneath her room.

As a matter of fact, the wine vaults of Mr. F., a wine merchant doing business the next door, extended under Mme. Hauffé's apartment, and Kerner, who was an old resident of the place, recognized from the seeress's description of her visitor a man who formerly was in Mr. F.'s employ as manager and bookkeeper. This man had died six years before, and had left something wrong with his accounts—in fact, there was a deficit of 1,000 florins, and the manager's private book was missing. The widow had been sued for the amount, and the matter was still unsettled. Again and again did this apparition come to Mme. Hauffé, bringing his paper and entreating her to interest herself in this affair. He declared that the necessary paper to clear up the whole matter was in a building sixty paces from her bed.

Mme. Hauffé said that in that building she saw a tall gentleman engaged in writing in a small room, which opened into a large one where there was a desk and chests; that one of the chests was open, and that on the desk was a pile of papers, among which she recognized the missing document.

The wine merchant, being present, recognized the office of the chief bailiff, who had the business in charge. Kerner went at once to the office and found everything as described, but, not finding the missing paper, concluded that her clairvoyance was at fault.

Mme. Hauffé, in her description of the paper said it had columns of figures upon it, and at the bottom was the number 80. Kerner prepared a paper corresponding to this description, and at the next séance presented it to her as the missing document. But she at once rejected it, saying the paper was still where she had before seen it.

On renewing the search the paper was found as described, and the bailiff was to bring it on the following day. He came accordingly. In her sleep, the seeress exclaimed:

"The paper is no longer in its place, but this is wonderful. The paper which the man always has in his hand lies open. Now I can read more: 'To be carried to my private book,' and that is what he always points to."

The bailiff was astonished, for instead of bringing the paper with him as Kerner had directed, he had left it lying open on his desk. All these things are attested by the bailiff, the wine merchant, Kerner, and others who witnessed them. Kerner himself visited the seeress more than a thousand times, and although during the first part of his observations he was skeptical, he was never able to detect her in the slightest attempt at deception. She was in no way elated over her peculiar power, on the contrary, she disliked to speak of it, and would gladly have been free from it altogether. Her clairvoyant powers were tested by hundreds of excellent observers during the last four years of her life.

The case of Alexis, the noted French somnambulist and clairvoyant, is worthy of notice here. I remember very well the account of a séance at a gathering of prominent Americans in Paris in 1853, of which the following is an abstract:—

Thick masses of cotton were bound firmly over his eyes in such a manner as to render it impossible for him to see in the ordinary way, and in this condition he described pictures, read signatures of letters folded in several envelopes, played games of cards with almost uniform success, and, being asked to select the best pianist in the room from a number present, who simply presented their hands for his inspection, he quickly selected a young man not yet eighteen years old, who had won four first prizes at the Conservatoire, and was really the best pianist of his age in Europe.

In playing cards he picked up the trick with a rapidity and certainty which showed how clearly he knew the position of the cards upon the table. Keeping those dealt to him in his left hand he held the card he intended to play in his right, and never once changed the card upon the play of his partner. He knew his adversary's hand as well as his own. The writer adds: "The cards used were bought by myself, half an hour before, so that any suspicion of prepared cards would be idle and absurd."

It remains to note some more recent instances reported by persons well known and specially qualified to judge of their truthfulness and value.

The first case which I will present is embodied in a report "On the Evidence of Clairvoyance," by Mrs. Henry Sidgwick, wife of Prof. Sidgwick, formerly president of the Society for Psychical Research. It was furnished by Dr. Elliott Coues of Washington, D. C., where the incident occurred, and was afterward investigated by Mr. F. W. H. Myers, secretary of the society. Both the persons participating in the incident were well known to Prof. Coues, and were both persons of prominence, one, Mrs. C., being well known as a writer and lecturer, and the other, designated as Mrs. B., was well known for her rare psychic faculties and her absolute integrity.

The incidents of the case are simple and unimportant, but they have a special value on account of their clearness, freedom from the possibility of external suggestion, and the well known ability and integrity of the reporter. The following are the points in the case:—

In Washington, D. C., January 14, 1889, between 2 and 3 o'clock P. M., Mrs. C., having been engaged in writing in the Congressional Library, left the building at 2:40 o'clock, and one or two minutes later was at her residence, in Delaware

Avenue, carrying her papers in her hand. In ascending the steps leading from the street to the front yard she stumbled and fell. She was not hurt, but "picked herself up" and went into the house.

About the same hour, certainly between 2 and 3 o'clock, Mrs. B., sitting sewing in her room a mile and a half away, sees the occurrence in all its details. The ladies are friends. They had met the day previous, but not since. The vision is wholly a surprise to Mrs. B. Nevertheless, it is so vivid that she at once sits down and writes to Mrs. C., describing minutely the occurrence, which letter Mrs. C. receives the next morning with much surprise. The following is an extract from the letter:—

"I was sitting in my room sewing this afternoon about 2 o'clock, when what should I see but your own dear self—but heavens! in what a position! You were falling up the front steps in the yard.

"You had on your black skirt and velvet waist, your little straw bonnet, and in your hand were some papers. When you fell, your hat went in one direction and your papers in another. You very quickly put on your bonnet, picked up your papers, and lost no time in getting into the house. You did not appear to be hurt, but looked somewhat mortified. It was all so plain to me that I had ten notions to one to dress myself and come over and see if it were true, but finally concluded that a sober, industrious woman like yourself would not be stumbling around at that rate, and thought I'd best not go on a wild-goose chase.

"Now, what do you think of such a vision as that? Is there any possible truth in it? I feel almost ready to scream with laughter whenever I think of it; you did look too funny spreading yourself out in the front yard. 'Great was the fall thereof.' I can distinctly call to mind the house in which you live, but for the life of me I cannot tell whether there are any steps from the sidewalk into the yard, as I saw them, or not."

In answer to Mr. Myers' letter of inquiry to Mrs. C., she says that the incident was described exactly—the dress as correctly as she could have described it herself. There were two steps from the sidewalk to the yard, and it was on the top one of these two steps that Mrs. C. stumbled. The manner of the fall, the behavior of the bonnet and papers, and her own sensations were all correctly described.

The next case—also embodied in the same report and examined in the same careful manner by Mr. Myers—was the exhibition of clairvoyant powers by a woman called Jane, the wife of a pitman in the County of Durham, in England. She received no fees and was averse to being experimented with for fear of being ridiculed or called a witch by her associates.

She was a particularly refined woman for one of her class, sweet, gentle, with delicately cut features, religious and conscientious to a remarkable degree. She was a marked example of those who, in the trance condition, could not be induced by suggestion to do a wrong or a mean act, or one which she would consider wrong in her normal state. In her sleep she was anæsthetic, felt herself quite on an equality with the operator, always spoke of herself as "we," and of her normal self as "that girl." The following instance of her clairvoyance was furnished by Dr. F., who knew her well for many years, and is from notes taken at the time:—

On the morning of the day fixed for the experiment the doctor arranged with a patient in a neighboring village that he should be in a particular room between the hours of 8 and 10 in the evening. The patient was just recovering from a severe illness and was weak and very thin and emaciated. This gentleman and the doctor were the only persons who knew anything of the arrangement or the proposed experiment.

After having secured the proper somnambulic condition in the subject, Dr. F. directed her attention to the house where his patient was supposed to be awaiting the experiment, as arranged. She entered the house, described correctly the rooms passed through, in one of which she mentioned a lady with black hair lying on a sofa, but no gentleman. The doctor's report then goes on as follows:—

"After a little she described the door opening and asked with a tone of great surprise:

"'Is that a man?'

"I replied, 'Yes; is he thin or fat?'

"'Very fat,' she answered; 'but has the gentleman a cork leg?'

"I assured her that he had not, and tried to puzzle her still more about him. She, however, persisted in her statement that he was very fat, and said that he had a great 'corporation,' and asked me whether I did not think such a fat man must eat and drink a great deal to get such a corporation as that. She also described him as sitting by the table with papers beside him, and a glass of brandy and water.

"'Is it not wine?' I asked.

"'No,' she said, 'It's brandy.'

"'Is it not whisky or rum?'

"'No, it is brandy,' was the answer; 'and now,' she continued, 'the lady is going to get her supper, but the fat gentleman does not take any.'

"I requested her to tell me the color of his hair, but she only replied that the lady's hair was dark. I then inquired if he had any brains in his head, but she seemed altogether puzzled about him, and only said she could not see any. I then asked her if she could see his name upon any of the papers lying about. She replied, 'Yes;' and upon my saying that the name began with E, she spelled each letter of the name, "Eglinton."

"I was so convinced that I had at last detected her in a complete mistake that I arose and declined proceeding further in the experiment, stating that, although her description of the house and the name of the person was correct, in everything connected with the gentleman himself she had told the exact opposite of the truth.

"On the following morning Mr. E., my patient, asked me the result of the experiment. He had found himself unable to sit up so late, he said, but wishful fairly to test the powers of the clairvoyante, he had ordered his clothes to be stuffed into the form of a human figure, and, to make the contrast more striking, he had an extra pillow pushed into the clothes, so as to form a 'corporation.' This figure had been placed by the table in a sitting position and a glass of brandy and water and the newspapers placed beside it. The name, he said, was spelled correctly, though up to that time I had been in the habit of writing it 'Eglington' instead of 'Eglinton.'"

Dr. Alfred Backman of Kolmar, Sweden, a corresponding member of the Society for Psychical Research and a good practical hypnotist has had unusually good fortune in finding clairvoyants among his own patients in that northern country. Two in particular, Anna Samuelson and Alma Redberg, gave most excellent examples of clairvoyant vision, describing rooms, surroundings, persons, and also events which were at the moment transpiring, though quite unknown and unsuspected by any one present at the experiment. Several of these cases are included in Mrs. Sidgwick's report. Instead of these cases, however, I prefer to adduce an instance or two reported by Dr. Dufay, a reputable physician of Blois and subsequently a senator of France. The cases were first reported to the French *Société de Psychologie Physiologique*, which was presided over by Charcot, and published in the *Revue Philosophique* for September, 1888.

Dr. Gerault, a friend of Dr. Dufay, had a maid-servant named Marie, who was a natural *somnambule*, but who was also frequently hypnotized by Dr. Gerault. Dr. Dufay witnessed the following experiments:—

Being hypnotized, Marie was describing to a young lady soon to be married, some characteristics of her lover, much to the amusement of the lady, who was clapping her hands and laughing merrily. Suddenly, almost with the rapidity of lightning, the scene changed from gay to grave. The somnambulist panted for breath, tears flowed down her face, and perspiration bathed her brow. She seemed ready to fall, and called on Dr. Gerault for assistance.

"What is the matter, Marie?" said the doctor; from what are you suffering?"

"Ah, sir!" said she; "ah, sir! how terrible! he is dead!"

"Who is dead? Is it one of my patients?"

"Limoges, the ropemaker—you know, in the Crimea—he has just died. Poor folks—poor folks!"

"Come, come, my child," said the doctor, "you are dreaming—it is only a bad dream.

"A dream," replied the somnambulist. "But I am not asleep. I see him—he has just drawn his last breath. Poor boy! Look at him."

And she pointed with her hand, as if to direct attention to the scene which was so vivid before her. At the same time she would have run away, but hardly had she risen to go when she fell back, unable to move. It was a long time before she became calm, but, on coming to herself, she had no recollection of anything which had occurred. Some time after, Limoges senior received news of the death of his son. It occurred near Constantinople on the same day that Marie had witnessed it in her clairvoyant vision.

On another occasion there was a séance at which ten or twelve persons were present. Marie was put to sleep and had told the contents of several pockets and sealed packages prepared for the purpose. Dr. Dufay came in late purposely, so as to be as much out of rapport with her as possible. He had just received a letter from an officer in Algiers, stating that he had been very ill with dysentery from sleeping under canvas during the rainy season. This letter he had placed in a thick envelope, without address or postmark, and carefully stuck down the edges. This again was placed in another dark envelope and closed in like manner. No one but himself knew of the existence of this letter.

Unobserved, he passed the letter to a lady present, indicating that it was to be given to Dr. Gerault, who received it without knowing from whom it came, and placed it in Marie's hand.

"What have you in your hand?" asked the doctor.

"A letter."

"To whom is it directed?"

"To M. Dufay."

"By whom?"

"A military gentleman whom I do not know."

"Of what does he write?"

"He is ill—he writes of his illness."

"Can you name his illness?"

"Oh, yes; very well. It is like the old woodcutter's of Mesland, who is not yet well."

"I understand; it is dysentery. Now listen, Marie. It would give M. Dufay much pleasure if you would go and see his friend, the military gentleman, and find out how he is at present."

"Oh, it is too far; it would be a long journey."

"But we are waiting for you. Please go without losing time."

(A long pause.) "I cannot go on; there is water, a lot of water."

"And you do not see any bridge?"

"Of course there is no bridge."

"Perhaps there is a boat to cross in, as there is to cross the Loire at Chaumont."

"Boats—yes—but this Loire is a regular flood; it frightens me."

"Come, come; take courage—embark."

(A long silence, agitation, pallor, nausea.) "Have you arrived?"

"Nearly; but I am much fatigued, and I do not see any people on shore."

"Land and go on; you will soon find some one."

"There, now I see some people—they are all women, dressed in white. But that is queer—they all have beards."

"Go to them and ask where you will find the military gentleman."

(After a pause.) "They do not speak as we do—and I have been obliged to wait while they called a little boy with a red cap, who understands me. He leads me on, slowly, because we are walking in sand. Ah! there is the military gentleman. He has red trousers and an officer's cap. But he is so very thin and ill. What a pity he has not some of your medicine!"

"What does he say caused his illness?"

"He shows me his bed—three planks on pickets—over wet sand."

"Thanks. Advise him to go to the hospital, and now return to Blois."

The letter was then opened and read to the company and caused no little astonishment.

Remarkable instances of clairvoyance have not been frequently reported in America. Nevertheless, well-authenticated cases are by no means wanting. Dr. S. B. Brittan, in his book entitled "Man and His Relations," relates several such cases. The following came under his own observation:—

In the autumn of 1855 he saw Mr. Charles Baker of Michigan, who, while out on a hunting excursion, had been accidentally shot by his companion. The charge passed through his pocket, demolishing several articles and carrying portions of the contents of the pocket deep into the fleshy part of his thigh. The accident was of a serious character, causing extreme suffering, great debility, and emaciation, lasting several months, as well as much anxiety regarding his ultimate recovery.

He was in this low condition when seen by Dr. Brittan. The doctor soon after returned East, and called on Mrs. Metler of Hartford, with whose clairvoyant power he was familiar, and requested her to examine into the condition of a young man who had been shot. No information was given as to his residence, condition, or the circumstances attending the accident.

She directly found the patient, described the wound, and declared that there was a piece of copper still in the wound, and that he would not recover until it was removed.

Young Baker, however, was sure he had no copper in his pocket at the time of the accident; the medical attendant found no indications of it, so it was concluded that the clairvoyant had made a mistake.

Later, however, a foreign substance made its appearance in the wound, and was removed by the mother of the patient with a pair of embroidery scissors; it proved to be a copper cent. The removal of the foreign substance was followed by rapid recovery. The discovery of the copper coin was made by the clairvoyant while at a distance of nearly one thousand miles from the patient.

Mrs. H. Porter, while at her home in Bridgeport, Conn., in the presence of the same writer, declared that a large steamer was on fire on the Hudson River; that among other objects in the vicinity she could clearly distinguish the village of Yonkers, and that the name of the steamer was the Henry Clay. The whole sad catastrophe was described by her with minuteness, as if occurring in her immediate presence.

The next morning the New York papers gave a full account of the burning of the Henry Clay off the village of Yonkers—an occurrence which, doubtless, some of my readers may still remember —corresponding in every important particular with that given by the clairvoyant.

Mr. John Fitzgerald of Brunswick, Me., once a somewhat noted temperance lecturer, but at the time now referred to a bed-ridden invalid, saw, clairvoyantly, and fully described the great fire in Fall River, Mass., in 1874, by which a large factory was destroyed. He described the commencement and progress of the fire, the means employed to rescue the operatives, criticised the work of the firemen, shouted directions, as if he were present, and at last as the roof fell in, he fell back upon the pillow and said:

"It is all over—the roof has fallen, and those poor people are burned."

It was not until three days later that Mrs. Fitzgerald obtained a paper containing an account of the fire. This she read to her husband, who frequently interrupted her to tell her what would come next as "he had seen it all." The account corresponded almost exactly with the description given by Mr. Fitzgerald while the fire was in progress.

I have, myself, recently found a very excellent subject whom I will call A. B., whom I first hypnotized on account of illness, but who afterward proved to have psychic perception and clairvoyant powers of a remarkable character. Once, while in the hypnotic condition, I asked her if she could go away and see what was transpiring in other places, as for instance, at her own home. She replied that she would try. I then told her to go to her home, in a small town three hundred miles away and quite unknown to me, and see who was in the house and what they were doing. After a minute of perfect silence she said: "I am there." "Go in," I said, "and tell me what you find." She said: "There is no one at home but my mother. She is sitting in the dining-room by a window; there is a screen in the window which was not there when I left home. My mother is sewing." "What sort of sewing is it?" I asked. "It is a waist for D." (her little brother). I wrote down every detail of her description, and then awoke her. She had no recollection of anything which had transpired, but said she had had a restful sleep. I then desired her to write at once to her mother and ask who was in the house at four o'clock this same afternoon, where she was, and what she was doing.

The answer came, describing everything exactly as set down in my notes.

On another occasion when I made my visit, it happened to be the day of the races occurring at a well known track some ten miles away, and members of the household where she was residing had gone to witness them. Neither she nor I had ever attended these races—we knew nothing of the appearance of the place, of the events that were expected, nor even of the ordinary routine of the sport. She was put into the deep hypnotic sleep, and thinking it a good opportunity to test her clairvoyance, I requested her to go to the grounds and I carefully directed her on her journey. Once within the inclosure she described the bright and cheerful appearance—the pavilion, the judge's stand, and the position of persons whom she knew. She said there was no race at the time; but that boys were going around among the spectators and getting money; that the people seemed excited; that they stood up and held out money, and beckoned to the boys to come—but she did not know what it meant. I suggested that perhaps they were betting. She seemed to look carefully and then said: "That is just what they are doing." She then described the race which followed, was much excited, and told who of the persons she knew were winners. I then said: "You will remember all this and be able to tell M. when she comes home."

It was found that everything had transpired as she had described. One of the races had been a failure, the horses coming in neck and neck; all bets were cancelled and new bets were made, which caused the excitement which she had witnessed. She surprised those who were present by the accuracy of her description, both of the place and the events, especially of the excitement caused by making the new bets.

On the same occasion, before awakening her, I said to her: "Now, I have something very particular to say to you and I want you to pay close attention.

"This evening when your dinner is brought up to you—you, A. B.'s second self, will make A. B. see me come in and stand here at the foot of the bed. I shall say to you: 'Hello! you are at dinner. Well, I won't disturb you,' and immediately I shall go. And you will write me about my visit." I then awoke her in the usual manner. This was Tuesday, July 3, 1894. On Thursday following I received this note, which I have in my possession.

"DEAR DR. MASON:—

"As I was eating my dinner on Tuesday I heard some one say 'Good-evening.' I turned around surprised, as I had heard no one enter the room, and there at the foot of the bed I saw *you*.

"I said 'Halloo! won't you sit down?' you said: 'Are you taking your dinner? Then I won't detain you,' and before I could detain you, you disappeared as mysteriously as you had come. Why did you leave so suddenly? Were you angry? Mary, the nurse, says you were not here at all at dinner-time. I say you were. Which of us is right?

"Sincerely,
"A. B."

(Full name signed.)

The clairvoyant faculty is sometimes exercised in sleep, and hence the importance so often attached to dreams. I have a patient, Miss M. L., thirty-five years of age, who has been under my observation for the past fifteen years, and for whose truthfulness and good sense I can fully vouch. From childhood she has been a constant and most troublesome somnambulist, walking almost every night, until two years ago when I first hypnotized her and suggested that she should not again leave her bed while asleep, and she has not done so.

This person's dreams are marvellously vivid, but her most vivid ones she does not call dreams. She says, "When I dream I dream, but when I see I see."

Nine years ago, M. L., had a friend in New Mexico whom I will call G., from whom she had not heard for months, and of whose surroundings she knew absolutely nothing.

One night she dreamed, or, as she expresses it, *saw* this friend in Albuquerque. She was, as it seemed to her, present in the room where he was, and saw everything in it with the same degree of distinctness as though she were actually present. She noticed the matting on the floor, the willow-ware furniture, bed, rocking-chair, footstool, and other articles. He was talking with a companion, a person of very striking appearance, whom she also minutely observed as regarded personal appearance, dress, and position in the room.

He was saying to this companion that he was about to start for New York for the purpose of interesting capitalists in a system of irrigation which he had proposed. His companion was laughing sarcastically and ridiculing the whole scheme. He persisted, and the conversation was animated—almost bitter.

Three weeks later, early one morning, she dreamed that this man was in New York. She saw him coming up the street leading to her house, and saw her father go forward to meet him. At breakfast she told her father her dream, and they also talked freely about her former dream or vision of three weeks before.

After breakfast her father sat upon the front stoop reading the morning paper, and M. L. went about some work. Suddenly she heard her father call out in a startled sort of way: "Mary, sure enough, here comes G.!" She stepped to the window and there was G. coming up the street and her father going forward to meet him exactly as she had seen him in her dream. He had just arrived from the West, and had come for the very purpose indicated by his conversation in M. L.'s vision. After some general conversation M. L. said to G; "By the way, who was that remarkable person you were talking with about this journey, three weeks ago?" mentioning the night of her dream. With evident surprise he said:

"What do you mean?"

She then related the whole dream just as she

had experienced it, even to the minutest details. His astonishment was profound. He declared that the details which she gave could never have been so exactly described except by some one actually present; and with some annoyance he accused her of playing the spy.

There are many other instances of remarkable clairvoyant vision on her part, and especially two which have occurred within the year—the visions having been fully described before the events were known.

Such are a few among hundreds of cases which might be adduced as examples of the clairvoyant power. They are from every period of history, from the earliest down to our own times. Looked at broadly, they at least show that a belief in the clairvoyant power of some specially endowed persons has existed throughout the historic period; they also exhibit a great similarity in their character and the circumstances under which they are observed.

Apollonius stops short in his discourse, apparently in his natural state, sees the assassination of Domitian, and shouts, "Strike the tyrant!"

Fitzgerald at Brunswick suddenly beholds the burning factories at Fall River, and shouts his orders to the firemen. Others spontaneously go into the somnambulic condition and only then become clairvoyant; while still others need the assistance of a second person to produce somnambulism and independent vision.

What is the nature and what the method of this peculiar vision which has been named clairvoyance?

Is it a quickening and extension of ordinary vision, or is it a visual perception obtained in some other manner, independent of the natural organ of sight?

It has been noted how vastly the action of the senses may be augmented by cultivation, but never has cultivation increased vision to such an extent as to discover a penny a thousand miles away and through opaque coverings. Besides, the clairvoyant vision is exercised quite independent of the bodily eye. The eyes may be closed, they may be turned upward or inward so that no portion of the pupil is exposed to the action of light, or they may be covered with thick pads of cotton or closed with plasters or bandages, yet the clairvoyant vision in proper subjects is obtained in just the same degree and with just the same certainty as when the eyes are fully exposed to the light.

It is true there has been much doubt and discussion on this vital point, the objectors maintaining that sight was possible and practicable by experts, notwithstanding the precautions used in blindfolding; in short, that the whole thing might safely be set down as deception and fraud.

In the face of facts such as are here cited, and the thousand others that might be adduced, it is hardly possible to treat this charge seriously.

To such objectors, cumulative evidence regarding facts out of their own mental horizon is useless. Their motto is: "No amount of evidence can establish a miracle;" and their definition of a miracle is something done, or alleged to have been done, contrary to the laws of nature. But the objector who refuses credence to well-attested facts on that ground alone, simply assumes that he is acquainted with all the laws of nature.

A miracle, really, is only something alleged to have been done, and we are not able to explain how; nevertheless, it may be perfectly in accordance with natural laws which we did not understand or even know existed. To the West Indian, whom Columbus found in the New World, an eclipse of the sun was a miracle of the most terrible character; to the astronomer it was a simple fact in nature. To the ignorant boor, "talking with Chicago" or cabling between New York and London is a miracle; to the electrician it is an everyday, well-understood affair. For a long time scientific men did not believe in the existence of globular, slowly-moving electricity; if such a thing had existed, it certainly should have put in an appearance before members of the "Academy," or "Royal Society" some time in the course of all these years; but it never had done so; only a few cooks, blacksmiths, or back-woodsmen had ever seen it, and they certainly were not the sort of people to report scientific matter; they did not know how to observe, and undoubtedly "they did not see what they thought they saw." But for all that, globular, slowly-moving electricity is now a well known fact in nature.

Neither the West Indian, the ignorant boor, nor the man of science had, at the time these several facts were presented to him, "any place in the existing fabric of his thought into which such facts could be fitted." The fabric of thought in each case must be changed, enlarged, modified, before the alleged facts could be received or assimilated.

The objector to the fact of clairvoyance and other facts in the new psychology is often simply deficient in the knowledge which would enable him properly to judge of these facts; he may be an excellent mathematician, physicist, editor, or even physician, but he has been educated to deal with a certain class of facts, and only by certain methods, and he is wholly unfitted to deal with another class of facts, perhaps requiring quite different treatment.

An excellent chemist might not be just the man to analyze questions of finance or to testify as an expert on the tariff, or a suspension bridge; the "texture of his thought" would need some modifying to fit him for these duties; indeed, he is fortunate if he can even be quite sure of morphia when he sees it; it might be a ptomaine.

If, then, the objector to well authenticated facts in any department of research expects his objections to be seriously considered, he must, at least, exhibit some intelligence in that department of research to which his objection relates.

I shall then simply reiterate the statement that there is abundant evidence of visual perception by some specially constituted persons, independent of any use of the physical organ of sight.

What the exact nature or method of this supranormal vision is, may not yet be absolutely settled, any more than the exact nature of light or of life or even of electricity is settled, and each of their various methods of action known, though of the fact itself in any of these cases there is no doubt.

From a careful consideration of the best authenticated facts and examples, we are led to believe that the faculty of clairvoyance is no supernatural gift, but may be possessed, to some degree, by many, perhaps by all, people; that it is a natural condition, developed and brought into exercise by a few, but undeveloped and dormant in most; that the faculty may include not only the power of obtaining visual perceptions at a distance and under circumstances which render ordinary vision impossible, but also the perception of general truth and the relation of things in nature to such a degree as to render the person who possesses it a teacher and prophet of seemingly supernatural endowments. Carefully excluding cases of unusual extension, or skill in using normal perceptive faculties, and also thought-transference, which, although bearing a certain relation to clairvoyance, should not be confounded with it, the phenomena of independent clairvoyance appear in certain persons under the following conditions :—

In certain states, brought about by disease, and at the near approach of death, in the hypnotic condition, whether self-induced or produced by the influence of a second person, and especially in the condition known as trance; it may also appear in sleep of the ordinary kind—in dreams, and especially in the condition of reverie or the state between sleeping and waking; a few persons also possess the clairvoyant faculty while in their natural condition, without losing their normal consciousness. In general it may be said that the faculty is most likely to appear when there exists a condition of abstraction, and the mind is acting without the restraint and guidance of the usual consciousness—and it reaches its most perfect exercise when this usual guidance ceases entirely—the body becoming inactive and anæsthetic and the mind acting independent of its usual manifesting organs. Such is the condition in trance.

This view is, of course, in direct opposition to the materialistic philosophy which makes the mind simply a "group of phenomena," the result of organization, and absolutely dependent upon that organization for its action, and even for its existence. To discuss this question here would occupy too much space; besides, one of the objects of these papers is to show this mind, spirit, psychos, mentality, "group of phenomena," what-

INDEPENDENT ACTION OF THE MIND. 115

ever it may be, and whatever name may be applied to it, acting under circumstances which will enable us to consider with greater intelligence this very question, viz.: Whether the mind, under some circumstances, is not capable of intelligent action independent of the brain and the whole material organization through which it ordinarily manifests itself.

CHAPTER V.

DOUBLE OR MULTIPLEX PERSONALITY.

IF there be any one thing in the empirical psychology of the past which has been considered settled past all controversy, it is the unity and continuity of human personality. Whatever might be believed or doubted concerning the after life, for this life at least believers and skeptics alike are united in the full assurance of a true, permanent, and unmistakable self. The philosopher Reid, a hundred years ago, in discussing this subject, wrote as follows :—

" My thoughts and actions and feelings change every moment. They have no continued but a successive existence, but that self or I to which they belong is permanent, and has the same relation to all succeeding thoughts, actions, and feelings which I call mine. The identity of a person is perfect—it admits of no degrees—and is not divisible into parts."

Now, while this dogma, which still expresses

the general consensus of mankind, may in a sense be well founded, still certain facts have been ascertained by the observant scouts in the outlying fields of psychology which, unless they can be interpreted to mean something different from their seeming and obvious import, make strongly against that stability and unquestioned oneness of human personality about which every individual in his own consciousness may feel so absolutely certain. What are these facts which have come to the notice of students of psychology?

The case of Félida X., reported by Dr. Azam of Bordeaux, is one of the earliest to attract the serious attention of medical men and students of psychology, and has become classic in relation to the subject.

She was a nervous child, given to moody spells and hysterical attacks, and, in 1856, when she was about fourteen years of age, she also began to have more serious attacks of an epileptiform character, from which she would emerge into a new and unusual condition, which was at first taken to be somnambulism. In this condition her general appearance was quite changed, and she talked and acted in a manner altogether different from her usual self. These attacks were at first very brief, lasting only a few minutes, but gradually they increased in duration until they occupied hours, and even days.

In her usual state she had no recollection and no knowledge whatever of her second condition, and the whole time spent in that condition was to her a blank; on the other hand, all the different occasions when she had been in this second condition were linked together, constituting a distinct chain of memories and a personality just as consciously distinct and conspicuous as her original self. In her second state she not only had the distinct memories connected with her own secondary personality, but she also knew facts concerning the first or original self, but only as she might have knowledge of any other person.

The two personalities were entirely different in character and disposition; the original one was sickly, indolent, and melancholy, while the new one was in good health, and in disposition bright, cheerful, and industrious. She married early in life, and was intelligent and efficient in the care of her family, rearing children and attending to the little business of a shop. At length this secondary self came to occupy nearly the whole time, and considered herself the normal personality, as, indeed, she was, being superior in every way to the original one. She knew very well how unhappy and miserable was the condition of the primary self, and, while she pitied her and did what she could to assist her, she disliked to have her return. She called the condition of the primary self, "that stupid state."

The lapses of the original or No. 1 personality became at length so frequent, or rather, so continuous, that she lost the proper knowledge and relation of things about her. She was a stranger in her own home, and on that account became still more morose and melancholy. To relieve as much as possible this distressing state of affairs the second self, or No. 2, when she knew that No. 1 was about to appear, would write her a letter, informing her of the general condition of the household, whom she might expect to meet, and where she would find certain needful articles; she would also offer advice regarding the conduct of affairs, which was always appropriate and useful and far superior to the judgment of the original self in the matters to which it referred.

As a second well marked and abundantly authenticated example of this divided or secondary personality, I will refer to a case in our own country and in our own vicinity.

Jan. 17th, 1887, Ansel Bourne, an evangelist, left his home in Rhode Island, and, after transacting some business in Providence, one item of which was to draw some money to pay for a farm for which he had bargained, he went to Boston, then to New York, then to Philadelphia, and, finally, to Norristown, Penn., fifteen or twenty miles from Philadelphia, where he opened a small store for the sale of stationery, confectionery, and five-cent articles. In this business he was known as A. J. Brown. He lived in a room partitioned off from the back of the store, eating, sleeping, and doing his own cooking there. He rented the store from a Mr. Earl, who also, with his family, lived in the building. Mr. Brown went back and forth to Philadelphia for goods to keep up his stock, and seems to have conducted his business as if accustomed to it.

Sunday, March 13th, he went to church, and at night went to bed as usual. On Monday, March 14th, about 5 o'clock in the morning, he awoke and found himself in what appeared to him an altogether new and strange place; he thought he must have broken into the place, and was much troubled, fearing arrest. Finally, after waiting two hours in great uneasiness of mind, he got up and found the door locked on the inside. He went out into the hall, and, hearing some one moving about, he rapped at the door. Mr. Earl, his landlord, opened it, and said: "Good-morning, Mr. Brown."

"Where am I?" said Mr. Brown.

"You are all right," replied Mr. Earl.

"I'm all wrong, and my name is not Brown. Where am I?"

"You are in Norristown."

"Where is Norristown?"

"In Pennsylvania, about seventeen miles west of Philadelphia."

"What day of the month is it?" inquired Mr. Brown.

"The 14th," replied Mr. Earl.

"Does time run backward here? When I left home it was the 17th."

"Seventeenth of what?" said Mr. Earl.

"Seventeenth of January."

"Now it is the 14th of March," said Mr. Earl.

Mr. Earl thought Mr. Brown was out of his mind, and sent for a physician. To the doctor he said his name was Ansel Bourne; that he remembered seeing the Adams Express wagons on Dorrance Street in Providence on Jan. 17th, and remembered nothing since, until he awoke here this morning, March 14th.

"These people," said he, "tell me that I have been here six weeks, and have been living with them all this time; I have no recollection of ever having seen one of them, until this morning."

His nephew, Mr. H., was telegraphed to in Providence.

"Do you know Ansel Bourne?"

Reply: "He is my uncle; wire me where he is, and if well."

Mr. H., went on to Norristown, took charge of his uncle and his affairs, sold out his store property, and Mr. A. J. Brown went back and resumed his life in Rhode Island as Ansel Bourne, but the time from Jan. 17th to March 14th was to him a blank.

Prof. James of Harvard and Dr. Hodgson, Secretary of the American Branch of the Society for Psychical Research, who reported this case to the society, now became interested in the matter. They went to see Ansel Bourne and learned the above history; but of the journey from Providence to Norristown in January no account of any kind could be obtained. Finally, he was put into the hypnotic condition, when he was again A. J. Brown, and gave a connected account of his journey to Boston, New York, Philadelphia, and of his stay in each of these cities; of his arrival at Norristown, and of his experience there up to the morning of March 14th, when everything was again confused. As A. J. Brown he knew of Ansel Bourne and of his remarkable history, but could not state positively that he had ever met him.

This transition was repeatedly made. Immediately on being put in the hypnotic trance and aroused to somnambulism he was A. J. Brown, a distinct personality, perfectly sane, and with a full appreciation of the relation of things as relating to that personality, and with a distinct chain of memories, beliefs, and affections; but, when introduced to the wife of Ansel Bourne, he entirely repudiated the idea of her ever having been his wife, though he might some time have seen her.

Immediately on being awakened from this hypnotic condition he was Ansel Bourne, with his usual consciousness, beliefs, affections, and chain of memories; but the primary Ansel Bourne personality had no knowledge whatever of the secondary, or A. J. Brown, personality, and for any act, either criminal or righteous, committed by the person A. J. Brown, the person Ansel Bourne had no more knowledge and consequently no more responsibility than for any good or bad action committed by a person in Australia and of whose existence he was ignorant.

A few other cases quite similar and in every

respect of equal interest have been observed, notably that known as Louis V., which was reported by Dr. Voisin of Paris and by several other well-known French physicians, under whose care from time to time he has been, and whose several reports have been summed up by Mr. Frederick W. H. Myers, the efficient London Secretary of the Society for Psychical Research.

Here the stability of personality was unsettled at the age of fourteen by a terrible fright from a viper. Four or five distinct personalities were represented.

(1) In his childhood, previous to his fright by the viper, he had good health and was an ordinary, quiet, obedient, well-behaved boy.

(2) A new personality, of which the primary self had no knowledge, was induced by the fright. This No. 2 personality had frequent epileptic attacks, but was able to work, learning the trade of a tailor.

(3) After one of these attacks of great violence, lasting fifty hours, another personality came to the surface—a greedy, violent, quarrelsome, drunken, thievish vagabond, paralyzed on one side, and with an impediment in his speech. He was an anarchist, an atheist, and a blackguard, always ranting and thrusting his opinions upon

those about him, perpetrating bad jokes, and practicing disgusting familiarities with his physicians and attendants. In this state, he knows nothing of the tailor's business, but he is a private of marines.

(4) He is a quiet, sensible man, retiring in behavior and modest in speech. If he is asked his opinions upon politics or religion, he bashfully replies that he would rather leave such things to wiser heads than his. In this condition he is without paralysis and speaks distinctly.

(5) As a man forty years of age he returns to the condition of childhood previous to his fright—a child in intellect and knowledge, having no occupation; he is simply an ordinary, quiet, well-behaved, obedient boy.

Each of these personalities was distinct from all the others; the earlier ones had no knowledge of those which came after them; the later ones had a knowledge of the earlier ones, but only as they might have knowledge of any other person.

A fourth typical case is that of Alma Z., recently reported by me for *The Journal of Nervous and Mental Diseases*. In this case, an unusually healthy, strongly intellectual girl, an expert in athletic sport and a leader wherever she might be, on account of overwork, and finally, of broken-down health, developed a second, and, later, a third personality. Each was widely different from the others, all were normal so far as a perfect knowledge of and adaptation to their surroundings were concerned, and all were of unusual intellectual force and brightness, as well as moral worth; but each was distinct, peculiar, and even in marked contrast to the others in many important characteristics. No. 1 had no knowledge of No. 2 nor of No. 3, except from circumstances and the report of others, and also from letters which passed between them giving information to No. 1 regarding changes which had occurred in her absence, as, for instance, of expected company or other engagement which it would be important for her to know.

Both of the later personalities were peculiarly fond of No. 1, and devoted to her welfare on account of her superior knowledge and admirable character. The case has been under my observation, both professionally and socially, for many years, and, in addition to its typical character, it presented an example of the singular fact of the persistence of the later personality, with the ability to observe, retain its chain of memories, and afterward report them, while the primary self was at the same time the dominant and active personality.

An instance of this occurred at one of the concerts of a distinguished pianist a few years since. No. 3 was the reigning personality, and she was herself a lover of music and an excellent critic. Beethoven's concerto in C major was on the programme, and was being performed in a most charming manner by soloist and orchestra. I was sitting near her in the box, when all at once I noticed a change in the expression of her face, which denoted the presence of No. 1. She listened with intense interest and pleasure to the performance, and at its close I spoke a few words to her, and she replied in her usual charming manner. It was No. 1 without doubt. Soon after, she leaned back in her chair, took two or three quick, short inspirations, and No. 3 was present again. She turned to me smiling and said:

"So No. 1 came for her favorite concerto; wasn't it splendid that she could hear it?"

I said: "Yes; but how did you know she was here?"

"Oh, I sat on the front of the box," she said. "I heard the music, too, and I saw you speaking to her."

The four cases here briefly outlined represent both sexes, two distinct nationalities, and widely-varying conditions in life. In each case one or more personalities crop out, so to speak, come to the surface, and become the conscious, active, ruling personality, distinct from the original self, having entirely different mental, moral, and even physical, characteristics; different tastes, and different sentiments and opinions; personalities entirely unknown to the original self, which no one acquainted with that original self had any reason to suppose existed in connection with that organization.

The cases present so many points of similarity in their history as to render it probable, if not certain, that some common principle, law, or mental state underlies them all—some law which, if clearly defined, would be valuable in reducing to order the seemingly lawless mass of phenomena which constantly meets us in this new and but little explored field of research.

It may be, also, that other mental states more frequently met with and more easily observed present points in common with these more striking and unusual ones; and that they also may assist us in finding the clue.

CHAPTER VI.

NATURAL SOMNAMBULISM—HYPNOTIC SOMNAMBULISM—DREAMS.

THE first of these more accessible conditions to claim attention is natural somnambulism, or sleep-walking. The phenomena of this peculiar state have been observed from time immemorial, and have always been looked upon as one of the most wonderful and interesting subjects in the domain of the old psychology.

In this state the subject, while apparently in ordinary sleep, arises from his bed and proceeds, sometimes to perform the most ordinary, every-day actions—cooking a dinner, washing clothes, sawing wood, or going out to a neighboring market town to transact business; sometimes, on the other hand, he does the most unusual things; he performs perilous journeys in dangerous and unfamiliar places in perfect safety and with unusual ease; sometimes intellectual work of a difficult nature, such as had baffled the student in his waking hours, is easily accomplished, and he finds the solution of his mathematical problem or the needed point in his argument all plainly wrought out and prepared for him when he goes to his desk the following morning; moreover, if the work from any cause should be interrupted, and the same conditions recur upon the following or some subsequent night, it may be resumed at the point where it was interrupted; or if the somnambulist talks, as well as acts, in his sleep the conversation shows that each succeeding occasion is connected with previous ones, all together constituting a chain of memories similar to that of the different personalities which have been presented in the four cases already described.

Sometimes all these different actions are accomplished without light or with the eyes fast closed, or else open and staring, but without vision. Sometimes, however, the new personality developed in the sleep of the somnambulist fails to come into proper relations with his surroundings, when he may also fail to accomplish the dangerous journey, and may walk from an open window or an unguarded balcony with disastrous results.

The second condition which presents analogies to the duplex or multiplex pesonalities, which are under consideration, is that of the somnambulism which occurs in the hypnotic sleep. While usually the hypnotic subject is passive and unconsciously receives the suggestions which are impressed upon him, not unfrequently a personality comes to the front which acts independently, and presents all the characteristics which we have found pertaining to a distinct personality.

A rare example of this alternating personality brought about by hypnotism is afforded by the French subject, Mme. B., whose acquaintance we have already made as a subject upon whom hypnotism at a distance was successfully carried out by Prof. Janet and Dr. Gibert of Havre. As we have already seen, in her ordinary condition Mme. B. is a stolid, substantial, honest French peasant, about forty years of age, of very moderate intelligence, and without any education or any ambition for notoriety. In this state Prof. Janet calls her Léonie.

Hypnotized, she is at once changed into a bright, vivacious, mischief-loving, rather noisy personality, who considers herself on excellent terms with the doctor, and whom the professor names Léontine. Later, by further hypnotization and a deeper trance, there appears a sedate, sensible personality, intellectually much superior to Léonie, the primary self, and much more dignified than the vivacious Léontine, and this third personality Prof. Janet calls Léonore.

Léontine, the hypnotic or second self, knows Léonie, the original Mme. B., very well, and is very anxious not to be confounded with her. She always calls her "the other one," and laughs at her stupidity. She says, "That good woman is not I, she is too stupid." One day Prof. Janet hypnotized Léonie, and as usual at once Léontine was present. Prof. Janet then suggested to Léontine that when she awoke and Léonie had resumed the command, she (Léontine) should take off the apron of Léonie, their common apron, on their one physical personality, and then tie it on again. She was then aroused from her hypnotic condition, and at once Léonie was present without the slightest knowledge of Léontine, for she never knew of this second personality, nor of hypnotic suggestion in any form. Léonie, supposing the professor's experiment was over, was conducting him to the door, talking indifferently in her slow, dull way, and at the same time unconsciously her fingers were working at her apron-strings. The loosened apron was falling off when the professor called her attention to it. She exclaimed, "Why, my apron is falling off!" and then, fully conscious of what she was doing, she replaced and tied it on again. She then continued her talk. She only supposed that somehow accidentally the apron had come untied and she had retied it, and that was all.

To the now submerged Léontine, however, this was not enough; her mission had not been completed, and at her silent prompting Léonie again fumbled at the apron-strings; unconsciously she untied and took off the apron, and then put it on again without her attention having been drawn to what she had now the second time done. The next day Prof. Janet again hypnotized Léonie and Léontine made her appearance.

"Well," said she, "I did what you told me yesterday. How stupid 'the other one' looked while I took her apron off! Why did you tell her that her apron was falling off? Just for that, I had to do the job all over again."

Here the hypnotic or secondary self, as in my own reported case, appears as a persistent entity, remembering and reasoning, while the primary self was at the same time in command of their common body. Léontine not only caused Léonie to untie and retie her apron, but she enjoyed the fun, remembered it, and told it the next day.

Again Léonore was as much ashamed of Léontine's flippancy as Léontine was of Léonie's stupidity.

"You see well enough," she said, "that I am not that prattler, that madcap. We do not resemble each other in the least."

In fact, she sometimes gave Léontine good counsel in regard to her behavior, and in a peculiar manner—by producing the hallucination of hearing a voice, thus again showing the conscious activity of the submerged self while a primary self was at the same time dominant and active. As Dr. Janet relates the incident, Léontine was one day in an excited, hysterical condition, noisy and troublesome with her chatter, when suddenly she stopped her senseless talk and cried out with terror:

"Oh! Who is it there talking to me like that?"

"No one was speaking to you."

"Yes, there on the left." And she opened a closet door in the direction indicated, to see that no one was hidden there.

"What is it that you hear?" asked the professor.

"I hear a voice on the left there which keeps saying to me: 'Enough, enough; be quiet. You are a nuisance!'" which, the professor remarks, was exactly the truth.

Léonore, in her turn, was then brought to the surface.

"What was it that happened," asked Prof. Janet, "when Léontine was so frightened?"

"Oh, nothing," she replied. "I told her she was a nuisance and to keep quiet. I saw she was annoying you. I don't know why she was so frightened."

I may be pardoned for mentioning one other fact regarding the relationship of these singular personalities, because it illustrates more pointedly if possible than anything else their entire duplex and separate character. Léonie or Madame B. is married, but Léontine is not. Madame B. however, was hypnotized at her accouchements, and became Léontine. So Léontine was the presiding personality when the children were born. Léontine therefore considers herself the mother of two children, and would be greatly grieved were any doubts expressed regarding her right of motherhood in them.

The analogies between the mental conditions presented respectively in ordinary somnambulism and the somnambulism of the hypnotic trance, and the mental conditions presented in the four cases previously recited are numerous and obvious; in fact, they seem as indeed they are, like the same conditions differently produced and varying in the length of time they occupy, and it is evident that in them there is brought to view a mental state of sufficient uniformity, as well as of sufficient interest and importance, to be worthy of serious consideration.

The facts thus far brought into view are these: That in a considerable number of persons there may be developed, either spontaneously or artificially, a second personality different in character and distinct in its consciousness and memories from the primary or original self; that this second personality is not a mere change of consciousness, but in some sense it is a different entity, having a power of observation, attention and memory not only when the primary self is submerged and without consciousness or volition, but also at the same time that the primary self is in action, performing its usual offices, and in its turn it is equally capable of managing the affairs and performing the offices properly pertaining to the common body whenever needed for that purpose.

Reckoning these different personalities as No. 1, No. 2, No. 3, etc., No. 1 has no knowledge of No. 2, nor of any succeeding personality, nor of their acts, but the time occupied by them is to No. 1 a blank, during which it is without volition, memory, or consciousness. No. 2 has a distinct consciousness and chain of memories of its own, but it also knows more or less perfectly the history and acts of No. 1—it knows this history, however, only as pertaining to a third person; it knows nothing of No. 3, nor of any personality subsequently coming into activity. No. 3 has also its distinct personality, and knows both No. 1 and No. 2, but knows them only as separate and distinct personalities; it does not know any personality coming into activity after itself.

So distinct are these personalities that No. 2 not only may not possess the acquirements, as, for instance, the book knowledge, trade, or occupation of No. 1, but may possess other capabilities and acquirements entirely foreign to No. 1, and of which it possessed no knowledge.

Ansel Bourne was a farmer and preacher, and knew nothing of storekeeping. A. J. Brown, the second personality, was a business man, neither farmer nor preacher. Louis V., as No. 2, was a tailor, and a very good boy; as No. 3, he was a private of marines, and knew nothing of tailoring, and he was a moral monster; while, in what might be called his No. 5 condition, he was again an undeveloped child, as he was before his fright.

Still another fact which comes prominently into

view in examining these cases is that the No. 2 personality may not, by any means, be inferior to the No. 1, or original self. In none of the cases cited has the intellectual capacity of the later developed personality been inferior to that of the original self, and generally it was notably superior; only in the No. 3 personality of Louis V. was the moral state worse than in No. 1, and, in general, the moral standing of No. 2 or No. 3 was fully equal to the primary self.

The emergence and dominance of a secondary personality, therefore, does not by any means imply that the general standing of the individual dominated by this second personality, as judged by disinterested observers, is in any way inferior to the same individual dominated by the primary self, but, on the contrary, a superior personality is rather to be expected, and especially is this true when the secondary personality is intelligently sought and brought to view by means of hypnotism.

It is, however, quite impossible by any *à priori* reasoning, or from the character of the primary self, to form any definite estimate concerning the character or general characteristics of any new personality which may make its appearance, either spontaneously or through the aid of hypnotism.

GENERAL CONSIDERATIONS. 139

Having become to a certain degree familiarized with the idea that in some persons, at least, and under some peculiar circumstances, a second personality may come to the surface and take the place for a longer or shorter time of the primary self, it may be asked whether, after all, these comparatively few persons in which this unusual phenomena has been observed are essentially different in their mental constitution from other people.

When those best acquainted with the slender and melancholy Félida X., or the ordinary, quiet, well-behaved Louis V.; the industrious and respected evangelist Ansel Bourne, or the large-brained, intellectual leader of women, Alma Z., saw them in their ordinary state, before any subliminal personality had emerged and made itself known, no one of those most intimate acquaintances, no expert in character-reading, no student of mental science could have given any reasonable intimation that any one of them would develop a second personality, much less give any trustworthy opinion as to the character which the new personality would possess.

A few months ago I was called in haste to see a patient, a large, strong man of one hundred and eighty pounds weight, who had been thrown down and trampled upon by his nineteen-year-old son during an attack of somnambulism, and had received such serious injuries as to require immediate surgical aid. The next day this son came to consult me regarding his unfortunate habit of sleep-walking, which has often got him into trouble before, and has now resulted in serious injury to his father. He is a slight youth of one hundred and twenty pounds weight, light hair, gray eyes, and a bright, frank face, expressive of good health and good nature—"a perfect gentleman," as his father expressed it, "when himself, but ten men cannot manage him when he gets up in his sleep; he will do what he sets out to do."

Who would ever imagine that this slender, good-natured, gentlemanly lad, sooner than any other lad, would in his sleep develop somnambulism and a second personality, or that when it came that second personality should prove a stubborn Samson?

Little could Prof. Janet imagine that beneath the surface consciousness of that serene and stupid Léonie dwelt the frisky, vivacious, fun-loving Léontine, waiting only the magic key of hypnotism to unlock and bring her to the surface to reign instead of the heavy Léonie.

The people who, in various ways, develop

second personalities may not differ, it seems, in any perceptible manner from other people; is it not quite possible, then, that other normal, ordinary people, possess a second personality, deep-down beneath their ordinary, everyday self, and that under conditions which favor a readjustment, this hidden subliminal self may emerge and become for a longer or a shorter time the conscious, acting one; and not only so, but may prove to be the brighter and better organized of the two?

Having now, as it were, a chart, imperfect though it be, of this outlying region, having some idea what to look for, and in what direction to look for it, it is possible that glimpses of this subliminal personality which each one unconsciously carries with him may be obtained under ordinary conditions and in everyday life, more frequently and more easily than we had imagined; for, as Ribot expresses it, the ordinary conscious personality is only a feeble portion of the whole psychical personality.

One example of this more usual form of double personality is afforded in ordinary dreaming. The dream country, like most of this outlying territory, has for the most part been studied without chart or compass. There is scarcely a point connected with the discussion of the subject upon which the most eminent authorities are not divided; it is Locke against Descartes, Hamilton against Locke, and Hobbes against the field.

If there be any one point, however, on which there is tolerable unanimity among all writers, ancient and modern, great and small, it is the absence in dreams of the normal acts and processes of volition, and, especially, of the faculty of attention. Now, this is exactly the condition which is conducive to the more or less perfect emergence and activity of the subliminal self, under whatever circumstances it occurs.

There is first, loss of consciousness from catalepsy, fright, depressing illness, hypnotism, or natural sleep, that is to say, the power of attention or volition in the primary self is abolished; then comes a readjustment of personalities, varying in completeness according to the ease with which, in different persons, this readjustment may be effected, and according to the completeness of the abolition of the power of attention and volition.

In sleep the conditions are favorable for this readjustment, and the subliminal self comes more or less perfectly to the surface; then appears that most peculiar and interesting series of pictures and visions which we call dreams: sometimes the rearranged, or rather unarranged, impressions and perceptions of the waking hours brought together, possibly just before the power of attention is entirely lost; sometimes the Puck-like work of the subliminal personality, the Léontines of the dream-country influencing the unconscious or semi-conscious primary self; sometimes the veridical or truth-telling dreams, which have been the wonder of all ages, and sometimes giving complete and active supremacy to the subliminal self as in natural somnambulism. Another portion of the field in which it might be profitable to look for evidence of the existence of a subliminal personality is in the eccentric work of genius; and still another, in the unexpected and often heroic actions of seemingly ordinary persons under the stress and stimulus of a great emotion, as of joy, sorrow, or anger, or of intense excitement, as for instance, the soldier in battle, the fireman at the post of danger, or the philosopher or astronomer on the eve of a new discovery; in all these cases the ordinary personality with its intense self-consciousness and self-considering carefulness is submerged—it disappears—the power of voluntary attention to mental states or physical action is lost; a new and superior personality comes to the surface and takes control. The supreme moment passes, and the primary self resumes sway, scarcely conscious of what has been done or how it was accomplished; even sensation has been abolished, and it is only now that he discovers the bleeding bullet-wound, the charred member, or the broken bone.

In physical science, whenever some new fact or law or principle has been discovered, it is at once seen that many things which before were obscure, or perhaps could only be accounted for by a theory of chance, or of direct interference by an omnipotent Deity, are now illuminated by a new light, and order reigns where before only confusion and darkness were visible. Something of the same sort is beginning to be recognized in the world of mental and psychical phenomena. If the mathematical exactness which measured the force of gravity, or placed the sun in one of the foci of an ellipse instead of the centre of a circle cannot be applied here, it is only on account of the vast complexity of the problem presented, and of which we know so few of the elements.

When matter alone is concerned we know exactly how it will act under given conditions. When life is added, the problem becomes more complex. The general law of evolution and the special law of natural selection in the development of species are accepted facts, although we cannot with success apply to them mathematical formulæ. When mind is added to life, the problem becomes still more complicated and mathematical exactness still less likely to be attained. Many facts, however, are being ascertained in psychical science, and some principles are being established which help to bring order out of confusion and shed light on some dark places.

The recognition of a subliminal self as forming a part of the psychical organization of man will throw light upon many obscure mental phenomena and bring order out of seemingly hopeless confusion. Placed before us as a working hypothesis, many other facts, before errant and unclassified, group themselves about it in wonderful clearness and harmony.

Granting, then, provisionally at least, the reality of the secondary self, what are its relations to the primary self and their common physical organization, and how came it to occupy these relations? Mr. Frederick W. H. Myers, to whom I have already referred, whose acute intellect and scholarly attainments have been of the highest value to the society in every department of its investigations, has also taken up this subject with his usual skill and judgment. He looks upon it from the standpoint of evolution, commencing with the earliest period of animal life. He compares the whole psychical organization, together with its manifesting physical organization, to the thousand looms of a vast manufactory.

The looms are complex and of varying patterns, for turning out different sorts of work. They are also used in various combinations, and there are various driving bands and connecting machinery by which they may severally be connected or disconnected, but the motive power which drives the whole is constant for all, and all works automatically to turn out the styles of goods that are needed.

"Now, how did I come to have my looms and driving-gear arranged in this particular way? Not, certainly, through any deliberate choice of my own. My ancestor, the ascidian, in fact, inherited the business when it consisted of little more than a single spindle; since his day my nearer ancestors have added loom after loom."

Changes have been going on continually; some of the looms are now quite out of date, have long been unused, and are quite out of repair or fallen to pieces. Others are kept in order because the style of goods which they turn out is still useful and necessary. But the class of goods called for has greatly changed of late. For instance, the machinery at present in operation is best adapted to turning out goods of a decidedly egoistic style, for self-preservation, persistence in the struggle for life, and for self-gratification; but a style is beginning to be called for of the altruistic pattern. For this kind of goods the machinery is not well adapted. It is old-fashioned, and changes are necessary. If there are any looms in the establishment unknown and unused which can be turned to account, or any way of modifying such as we have to meet the demand, it is for our interest to know it.

But the methods of adjustment, and arrangements for bringing new looms into operation are hidden and difficult of access, so we observe factories where spontaneous readjustments are going on and new looms, not known to have been in the establishment, are being brought automatically into action and are found to work fairly well. Such instances are found in the establishment of Félida X. or Louis V., from which valuable hints are obtained regarding changes and readjustments.

Furthermore, in hypnotism, we find a safe and, at the same time, powerful lever, for readjustment, by means of which in some establishments new looms can be brought into play and shut off again almost at will; and often while the new looms are at work doing good service we are able to get at the old ones, repair and modernize them so as to make them useful, and the immense value of hypnotism in this educational and reformatory work has hardly begun to be known or appreciated. A single instance out of many must suffice for illustration.

In the summer of 1884 there was at the Salpêtriére a young woman of a deplorable type, Jeanne S., who was a criminal lunatic, filthy, violent, and with a life history of impurity and crime. M. Auguste Voisin, one of the physicians of the staff, undertook to hypnotize her May 31st. At that time she was so violent that she could only be kept quiet by a strait-jacket and the constant cold douche to her head. She would not look at M. Voisin, but raved and spat at him. He persisted, kept his face near and opposite to hers, and his eyes following hers constantly. In ten minutes she was in a sound sleep, and soon passed into the somnambulistic condition. The process was repeated many days, and gradually she became sane while in the hypnotic condition, but still raved when she awoke.

Gradually, then, she began to accept hypnotic suggestion, and would obey trivial orders given her while asleep, such as to sweep her room, etc.; then suggestions regarding her general behavior; then, in her hypnotic condition, she began to express regret for her past life and form resolutions of amendment, which she fully adhered to when she awoke. Two years later she was a nurse in one of the Paris hospitals, and her conduct was irreproachable. M. Voisin has followed up this case by others equally striking.

Such is an imperfect sketch of the discoveries, experiments, and studies which have been made in the domain of human personality. It is merely a sketch, and certainly it is in no spirit of dogmatism that it is presented; but as a collection of facts relating to human nature and the constitution and action of the human mind, it is at least curious.

It need not destroy our convictions regarding the essential unity of personality, but it must necessarily enlarge our conceptions of what *constitutes an individual*, and how under various circumstances that individual may act.

From many points of view, and in relation to many departments of study and of human development—legal, moral, social, and educational

—the subject presents important bearings; and, furthermore, in the solution of other psychological problems it will be found to possess the greatest possible interest and value.

CHAPTER VII.

AUTOMATISM—PLANCHETTE.

OUR ordinary actions, both physical and mental, are, for the most part, subject to our own voluntary guidance and choice. Of this, at least, we feel sure. We work, walk, talk, play upon an instrument, read a book, or write a letter, because we choose to do these things; and ordinarily they are done under the full guidance of our will and intelligence. Sometimes, however, actions are performed by us without our choice or guidance, and even without our consciousness, and such actions are called automatic. The thrifty housewife, perhaps also being of a literary turn of mind, may become deeply absorbed in an exciting novel, while at the same time her busy fingers, without thought or effort on her part, skilfully ply the knitting needles, or her well accustomed foot, with gentle motion, rocks the cradle.

During an exciting conversation, or the absorbing consideration of some important subject or problem, the act of walking is performed without will or consciousness; the pianoforte player runs his scales and roulades with marvellous rapidity and precision while reading a book or carrying on an animated conversation. Such actions are performed automatically.

When we come to examine a large number of actions performed in this automatic manner, we observe that they exhibit great diversity in the kind and degree of automatism displayed in their performance. In the cases above mentioned the mind is simply altogether engaged in doing one thing, and at the same time the muscles go on without any conscious direction or supervision, doing altogether another thing, but generally something which they had before been accustomed to do. This is often called absent-mindedness; it is also one of the most common and simple forms of automatism. We set the machine to work, and it goes itself.

Another kind of automatism is that which often appears in connection with peculiar gifts or talents, and is especially associated with genius. It is seen, for example, in the poet and the orator, and in those capable of improvisation, especially in music or in verse. The pianist or organist seats himself at the instrument without the remotest idea of what he is to perform—he simply commences. The theme he is to present, the various melodies, harmonies, changes, and modulations which come at his touch are often as much a surprise and delight to himself as to the most interested listener. Something within him furnishes and formulates the ideas, and causes him to express them artistically upon the instrument of his choice without any effort, or even supervision of his own—he is simply conscious of what is produced—but if he should undertake consciously to guide or in any way interfere with the production, the extraordinary beauty and excellence of the performance would at once cease.

Still another kind of automatism is illustrated in somnambulism. The somnambulist arises from his bed in his sleep, and proceeds to prepare a meal or work out a mathematical problem or write a thesis or a letter, or sometimes to describe distant scenes and events transpiring far away. Here the actions, both physical and mental, are performed, not only without the exercise of the actor's own choice or control, but he has no knowledge of them whatever. They are altogether outside the domain of his consciousness, and have their origin in some centre of intelligence quite apart from his own ordinary consciousness, and they only appear or find expression through his physical organization. Let us examine a little more closely into these different forms of automatism.

Twenty-five years ago a curious little piece of mechanism—apparently half toy and half an instrument for amateur conjuring—made its appearance in the windows of the toyshops and bookstores of the United States. It was a little heart-shaped piece of mahogany, or other hard wood, about seven inches by five in dimensions, with two casters serving for feet at the base of the heart, while a closely-fitting pencil passed through a hole at the point or apex.

Thus a tripod was formed, moving with perfect ease and freedom in any direction, while the pencil, which formed the third foot, left its plain and continuous tracing wherever the instrument was moved.

This little toy was called Planchette, and wonderful tales were told of its strange performances when rightly used. Evenly adjusted upon a plain wood table, if a properly-constituted person placed his or her finger-tips lightly upon its surface, it soon began to move about, without any muscular effort or any wish or will on the part of the operator; a broad, smooth sheet of paper being placed beneath it upon the table, figures, words, and sentences were plainly traced by the pencil, all in the style of a veritable oracle, and greatly to the delight of the curious, the wonder of the superstitious, and the mystification of people generally.

Not every one, however, could command the services of the modern oracle; only to the touch of a certain few was it responsive; to the many it was still and silent as a sphinx. One in ten, perhaps, could obtain a scrawl; one in twenty, intelligible sentences, and one in a hundred could produce remarkable results. Few persons witnessing its performances under favorable circumstances failed to be interested, but different people looked at it from quite different standpoints. The habitual doubter saw in it only a well-managed trick, which, however, he failed to detect; the spiritualist saw undoubted evidence of spiritual manifestations, while the great majority of common-sense people saw writing done, evidently without will or effort on the part of the writer, producing messages of every grade, from the most commonplace twaddle, foolishness, and even falsehood, to the exhibition of intelligence of a high order, a sparkling wit, and a perception of events, past, present, and sometimes even of those still in the future, most acute and unusual. What was the cause of these involuntary movements, or whence came the messages written, they did not know, and few even cared to speculate.

That was twenty-five years ago, and the two theories already alluded to were about the only ones adduced to account for the phenomena. Dr. Carpenter's theory of "unconscious cerebration" and "unconscious muscular action" did not cover the ground; there was altogether too much cerebration not to have a consciousness connected with it in some way. The theory did not cover the facts. Twenty-five years have failed to detect the long-talked-of trick of the skeptic; they have also failed to substantiate the claim of spiritualists, and Planchette-writing is almost as much a mystery as ever.

Fairly studied, then, what does Planchette really do? From a physical standpoint its performances are simply automatic writing or drawing. To deny the automatic character of the movements of Planchette at this day is simply absurd. That writing can be produced with it voluntarily, no one doubts, but that it generally is produced automatically, that is, without the choice or control of the writers, and without their knowledge of what is being written, it would be waste of time here to attempt to prove; the theory of fraud is untenable, and the real question at issue is the psychical one, namely, whence come the messages which it brings?

These messages may be divided into three general classes: (1) Those which are trivial or irrelevant. (2) Those which show intelligence and have some unmistakable relation to the subject of which they purport to give information, but all of which is known either to the writers or some person present. (3) Those which bring, or profess to bring, information unknown in any way, either to the writer or any person present.

The first of these divisions need not detain us, though it contains a very large share of all the messages received, as it simply illustrates the fact of automatism, which is equally well illustrated in the other classes of messages, which are of a more interesting character. The second class, namely, messages which show intelligence and have an unmistakable relation to the subject concerning which information is asked, and yet contain nothing beyond the knowledge of the writers or of persons present, is also very large.

The following is a sketch of my own first experience with Planchette. I may remark that subsequent trials brought out the fact that for myself alone Planchette will do nothing; it will not even move a hair's-breadth; but when, as is often the case, two persons are needed for success, I am often selected by Planchette to assist when it is consulted in the matter. On one occasion, I was calling at a friend's house, in the spring of 1868. Planchette was then much in vogue, and one stood on a side-table in the room. A young daughter of my friend—a school-girl fifteen or sixteen years of age—remarked that Planchette would move and sometimes even write for her, and she asked me to join her in a trial. I consented, and, to our surprise, the moment our fingers were placed lightly upon the instrument it moved off with great energy. Questions were then asked, and the answers were written with promptness and intelligence, greatly to the amusement of the company. Desiring to know who our mysterious correspondent might be, we politely said, "Planchette, will you kindly inform us who it is that writes these answers?" to which it replied, "Peter Stuyvesant."

"Old Governor Stuyvesant?" we asked.

"Yes," was the reply.

Now it so happened that a short time previous to our séance the old pear tree, known as the Stuyvesant pear tree, which had stood for more than two hundred years at the corner of Thirteenth Street and Third Avenue, having become decayed and tottering, was thrown down by a blow from a passing truck and had been ruthlessly chopped to pieces by workmen; and the event had been generally noticed and commented upon. Accordingly we replied,

"We are very glad to hear from you, Governor. How about the old pear tree?"

To this a reply was promptly written, but neither of us had the slightest idea what it might be. The young lady took up the paper and commenced to read, but was shocked and greatly confused to find, clearly written, in a hand quite foreign to us both, "It's a —— —— shame!" the blanks here being filled by the most emphatic expletives, and without the slightest abbreviation.

Another excellent Planchette-writer was Miss V., a friend of the family, who was spending a few days at my house in March, 1889. She was a young German lady of unusual intelligence, vivacity, and good sound sense. She knew of spiritualism only by passing remarks which she might have heard, and had never either seen or heard of Planchette. She was herself a somnambulist, or, rather, a somniloquist, for she never walked in her sleep, but talked with the greatest ease, carrying on long conversations without the slightest memory afterwards of what had been said. She was also an excellent hypnotic subject, and the suggested effects of medicines were much more prompt and certain than the effect of the medicines themselves, when used in the ordinary way.

For experiment one evening I proposed that we should try Planchette. As soon as our fingers were placed upon the instrument, it moved off across the table with the greatest promptness, and at once it replied to questions with unusual appropriateness and intelligence. The astonishment of Miss V. was altogether too profound and too apparent to admit of any suspicion of collusion on her part, and she had seen that the board would not move for me alone, yet she could not be persuaded that when we wrote together there was not some trick, and that I did not move the board voluntarily to produce the writing.

At length a message came concerning one of her own relatives, of whom she was sure that I could have no knowledge whatever, and she was convinced that at all events that message could not have originated with me. Accordingly she became a most valuable and interested partner in the experiments, and the chief medium through whom Planchette gave its communications.

Our sittings continued four or five consecutive evenings, and hundreds of communications and answers to questions were given by different intelligences or personalities, with entirely different modes of expression and different kinds of writing; some were religious, some philosophical, some were anxious to give advice, and some were profane; this last-mentioned phase appearing especially if we were persistent in inquiring too closely into the identity and former condition of the communicating personality.

On one occasion a message was written which was so strange in its appearance that none of us could at first make it out. At length we discovered some familiar negro phrase, and applying this key, we found we had a message of regular plantation negro talk, bearing a very strong resemblance to Uncle Remus's talk to the little boy, which some of us had just been reading. On asking who the "intelligence" was, it wrote, "Oh, I'se a good ole coon."

"Neither Miss V. nor myself had ever heard such a dialect spoken, nor knew that any sort of person of the negro race was ever called a "coon."

On another occasion, Miss V. was anxious to know and asked Planchette if a relative of hers, whom she named, was staying in town that night. The answer came, "Yes." "Where is he stopping?" Answer: "At the H. House." "What is he doing now?" Answer: "He has just finished his dinner, settled his bill at the cashier's desk, and is now walking up Broadway with his cousin." She afterward learned that this information was correct in every particular.

On the last evening of our experiments the force displayed in the writing was something surprising. Miss V. always experienced a certain amount of pain in her arms while writing, as if she were holding the electrodes of a battery through which a mild current was passing. On this occasion the pain was almost unbearable, so that she frequently cried out, and was obliged to remove her hands from the board for relief.

The writing was so violent that it could be heard in the next room, and at times it seemed as though the board would surely be broken. Seeing so much force exhibited, I allowed my fingers merely to touch the surface of the board, but so lightly that my hands did not move with it at all, but simply retained contact, the board sliding along beneath them. The writing continued with just the same violence. I then called the attention of Miss V. to what I was doing, and requested her to adjust her hands in a similar manner. She did so, and the instrument continued to write several words, with gradually diminishing force, moving under our hands, while our hands did not follow at all the movements of the instrument, until at length it gradually stopped, like a machine when the power is turned off.

Miss V. does not reside in the city, but while I was writing this chapter she was in town, and spent a few hours at my house. We were both anxious to try Planchette again. When we placed our fingers upon the board, the writing commenced at once, and intelligent answers were given to about twenty questions, some of the answers, especially those relating to distant friends, being quite contrary to our impressions and our hopes, but they were afterward found to be true.

We remembered the experiment just related, which was made more than four years ago. The force on this occasion was not at all to be compared with what it was then, but we said, "Now, Planchette, we want to ask a favor of you; will you repeat the experiment of four years ago, and move under our hands, while our hands remain stationary?" It replied, "Since you are so polite, I will try; perhaps I can move it a little."

We then planted our elbows firmly upon the table, curved our wrists, so as to allow the tips of our fingers to rest in the lightest possible manner upon the surface of the board. Four of us were watching with great interest for the result. After a moment's hesitation, slowly the board moved nearly an inch and stopped, but the movement was so obvious and decided, and without any movement of our hands, that a simultaneous shout went up from us all, and "Well done, Planchette!" The experiment was successfully repeated several times, the tracing of the pencil in each case showing a movement of from one to two inches.

A most valuable series of experiments in Planchette-writing was recently carried on by the late Rev. Mr. Newnham, vicar of Maker, Davenport, England, a member of the Society for Psychical Research, together with his wife. They were fully reported to Mr. F. W. H. Myers, secretary of the society.

The experiments extended over a period of eight months, and more than three hundred questions and answers were recorded. Mrs. Newnham alone was the operator, and the important peculiarity in these experiments was, that although quite in her normal condition, yet in no instance here related did she see the question written to which she wrote the answer, nor did she hear it asked, nor did she have any conscious knowledge, either of question or answer, until the answer was written and read. She sat upon a low chair at a low table some eight or ten feet from her husband, while he sat at a rather high table, with his back to her. In this position he silently wrote out the questions, it being impossible for her to see either the paper, the motion of his hand, or the expression of his face, and their good faith, as well as that of many intelligent witnesses, is pledged to the truth of this statement.

Mr. Newnham remarks that Planchette commenced to move immediately upon the first trial, and often the answer to questions prepared as just described was commenced before the question was fully written out.

At their first sitting, finding that the instrument would write, he proposed, silently, in writing, six questions, three the answers to which might be known to Mrs. Newnham, and three relating to his own private affairs, and of which the answers could not have been known to her. All six were immediately answered in a manner denoting complete intelligence, both of the question and the proper answer. He then wrote: "Write down the lowest temperature here this winter." Answer: "8." The actual lowest temperature had been 7·6 degrees, so 8 was the nearest whole degree, but Mrs. Newnham remarked at once that had she been asked the question she should have written 7, and not 8, because she did not remember the fraction, but did remember that the figure was 7 something.

Again it was asked, "Is it the operator's brain, or an immaterial spirit that moves Planchette? Answer 'brain' or 'force.'"

"Will."

"Is it the will of a living person or of an immaterial spirit? Answer 'force' or 'spirit.'"

"Wife."

"Give, first, the wife's Christian name, and then my favorite name for her." This was accurately done.

"What is your own name?"

"Only wife."

We are not quite sure of the meaning of your answer. Explain."

"Wife."

"Who are you that writes?"

"Wife."

"Does no one tell wife what to write? If so, who?"

"Spirit."

"Whose spirit?"

"Wife's brain."

"But how does wife's brain know certain secrets?"

"Wife's spirit unconsciously guides."

"Can you foresee the future?"

"No."

On another occasion it was asked: "Write out the prayer used at the advancement of a Mark Master Mason."

"Answer: Almighty Ruler of the Universe and Architect of all Worlds, we beseech Thee to accept this, our brother, whom we have this day received into our most honorable company of Mark Master Masons. Grant him to be a worthy member of our brotherhood, and may he be in his own person a perfect mirror of all Masonic virtues. Grant that all our doings may be to Thy honor and glory and to the welfare of all mankind."

Mr. Newnham adds: "This prayer was written off instantaneously and very rapidly. I must say that no prayer in the slightest degree resembling it is made use of in the ritual of any Masonic degree, and yet it contains more than one strictly accurate technicality connected with the degree of Mark Master Mason. My wife has never seen any Masonic prayers, whether in 'Carlile,' or any other real or spurious ritual of the Masonic Order."

The whole report shows the same instantaneous appreciation of the written questions, by the intelligence and appropriateness with which the answer was framed, though Mrs. Newnham never had any idea what the question was until after the answer was written and read, and the answers very often were entirely contrary to the prejudices and expectations of both the persons engaged in the experiments.

The following case may fairly be placed in the third class of messages, namely, those conveying intelligence which seems to be beyond the possible knowledge of the writer or of any person present. It is a well authenticated and interesting example of Planchette-writing, reported to Mr. Myers, the reporter being Mr. Hensleigh Wedgwood, a cousin and brother-in-law of Charles Darwin, and himself a savant of no small reputation. Two ladies, sisters, whom he designates as Mrs. R. and Mrs. V., were for many years intimate and valued friends of Mr. Wedgwood, and it was in co-operation with one or the other of these ladies that the results to be noted, along with much other interesting matter, were obtained.

Sitting alone, neither of the ladies nor Mr. Wedgwood was able to obtain any results at all with Planchette; the board remained absolutely motionless. The two ladies together could obtain no writing, but only wavy lines, made rapidly, like a person writing at full speed, but with Mr. Wedgwood co-operating with either of the ladies the writing was intelligible, but was much stronger and more vivacious with Mrs. V. than with Mrs. R. The following extracts are from Mrs. R.'s journal of a sitting, June 26, 1889:

"With Mr. W. and Mrs. R. at the board, Planchette writes: 'A spirit is here who thinks he will be able to write, through the medium. Hold very steady, and he will try first to draw.' We turned the page, and a sketch was made, rudely enough, of course, but with much apparent care. Planchette then wrote:

"'Very sorry can't do better; was meant for test; must write for you instead. (Signed) J. G.'

"We did not fully understand this drawing; and Mr. W. asked, 'Will J. G. try again?' which it did. Below the drawing it wrote: 'Now look.' We did, and this time clearly comprehended the arm and sword. Mr. W. asked, 'What does the drawing represent?'

"'Something given to me.'

"Mrs. R. asked, 'Are you a man or a woman?'

"'A man—John G.'

"Mr. W. asked, 'How was it given to you?'

"'On paper and other things.'

"Mr. W. 'We don't know J. G. Have you anything to do with us?'

"'No connection.'

"Mr. W. said he knew of a J. Gifford, and wondered if that was the name.

"'Not Gifford; Gurwood.'

"Mr. W. suggested that he had been killed in storming some fort.

"'I wish I had died fighting.'

"'Were you a soldier?'

"'I was in the army.'

"'Can you say what rank?'

"'No; it was the pen did for me, not the sword.'

"We suggested that he was an author who had failed or been maligned.

"'I did not fail. I was not slandered. Too much for me after—the pen was too much for me after my wound.'

"Asked to repeat, it wrote: 'I was wounded in the Peninsula. It will be forty-four years next Christmas Day since I killed myself—I killed myself. John Gurwood.'"

Leaving Mrs. R.'s diary, the following is the account Mr. Wedgwood wrote of the séance at the time:—

"JUNE 26, 1889.—Had a sitting at Planchette with Mrs. R. this morning. Planchette said there

was a spirit there who thought it could draw if we wished it. We said we should be glad if he would try. Accordingly Planchette made a rude attempt at a hand and arm proceeding from an embattled wall and holding a sword. A second attempt made the subject clearer. Planchette said it was meant for a test. The spirit signed it 'J. G.' No connection of ours, he said. We gradually elicited that his name was John Gurwood, who was wounded in the Peninsula in 1810, and killed himself on Christmas Day, 1845. It was not the wound but the pen that did it.

"JULY 5, 1889.—I made the foregoing memorandum the same day, having very little expectation that there would be any verification.

"H. WEDGWOOD."

Quoting again from Mrs. R.'s journal: "Friday, Sept. 27.—Mr. Wedgwood came, and we had two sittings—in the afternoon and evening. I think the same spirit wrote throughout, beginning without signature, but when asked the name, writing John Gurwood. The effort, at first incoherent, developed afterward into the following sentences: 'Sword—when I broke in, on the table with plan of fortress—belonged to my prisoner—I will tell you his name to-night. It was on the table when I broke in. He did not expect me. I took him unawares. He was in his room, looking at a plan, and the sword was on the table. Will try and let you know how I took the sword to-night.'

"In the evening, after dinner: 'I fought my way in. His name was Banier—Banier—Banier. The sword was lying on a table by a written scheme of defence. Oh, my head! Banier had a plan written out for defence of the fortress. It was lying on the table, and his sword was by it.

". . . Look! I have tried to tell you what you can verify.'"

Mr. Wedgwood reports his verification as follows:—

"When I came to verify the messages of Planchette, I speedily found that Col. Gurwood, the editor of the duke's dispatches, led the forlorn hope at the storming of Ciudad Rodrigo in 1812 (note Planchette's error in date), and received a wound in his skull from a musket-ball, 'which affected him for the remainder of his life,' (*Annual Register*, 1845). In recognition of the bravery shown on that occasion, he received a grant of arms in 1812, registered in the College of Arms as having been passed 'upon the narrative that he (Capt. G.) had led the forlorn hope at Ciudad Rodrigo, and that after the storming of the fortress the Duke of Wellington presented him with the sword of the governor who had been taken prisoner by Capt. Gurwood.'"

The services thus specified were symbolized in the crest, described in the "Book of Family Crests": "Out of a mural coronet, a castle ruined in the centre, and therefrom an arm in armor embowed, holding a cimeter."

It was evidently this crest that Planchette was trying to sketch. The *Annual Register* of 1845 also confirms Planchette's assertion that Col. Gurwood killed himself on Christmas Day of that year, and adds: "It is thought that this laborious undertaking (editing the dispatches) produced a relaxation of the nervous system and consequent depression of spirits. In a fit of despondency the unfortunate gentleman terminated his life." Compare Planchette: "Pen was too much for me after the wound."

Here are described four instances of automatic writing by means of Planchette. Two of these cases were reported to Mr. Myers, who has thoroughly canvassed them as regards their authenticity, as well as the ability and good faith of the persons concerned, both in the writing and reporting; and he has made use of them in his own able argument upon the same subject.

In the other cases the messages were written under my own observation, my own hands also being upon the board. In the case of Mr. and Mrs. Newnham the intelligence which furnished the messages disclaimed altogether the aid of any spirit except "wife's spirit," which did "unconsciously guide." In the case reported by Mr. Wedgwood and Mrs. R., the intelligence distinctly claimed to be from Col. John Gurwood, who had died nearly fifty years before. In my own cases, in that written with the co-operation of my friend's school-girl daughter, the intelligence claimed to be that of Peter Stuyvesant, while in those written with Miss V., various names were given, none of which was recognized as belonging to a person of whom we had ever had any knowledge, and all bore abundant evidence of being fictitious. One, indeed, professed to be "Beecher," and declined to give an opinion on the prospective trotting qualities of a colt, on the ground that he was "no horseman"; and in our later experiments, when closely questioned, it distinctly stated that the intelligence came from the mind of Miss V. herself.

Let us analyze these messages a little further. Those written by Mr. and Mrs. Newnham were remarkable, not only because Mrs. Newnham was writing without any conscious knowledge of what was being written, but neither had she any conscious knowledge of the questions to which she was writing the answers. Evidently, then, her own ordinary consciousness was not acting at all in the matter regarding either the questions or answers, for she was fully awake, in her normal condition, and perfectly competent to judge of her own mental state and actions. Nevertheless, there was some intelligence acting reasonably and consciously, and making use of her hand to register its thoughts.

In a former chapter I have described and illustrated a somewhat unusual mental phenomenon, to which the name thought-transference, or telepathy, has been given; and in another I have endeavored to demonstrate the existence of a secondary or subliminal self or personality.

If I mistake not, it is here, in these two comparatively little known and, until recently, little studied, psychical conditions, that we shall find the key to message-bearing automatism, as well as other manifestations of intelligence which have heretofore been considered mysterious and occult. Applying this key to the Newnham Planchette-writing, the secondary personality or subliminal self of Mrs. Newnham took immediate cognizance of the questions silently and secretly written out by her husband, although they were utterly unknown to her ordinary or primary self, and made use of her hands to communicate the answer.

The answer, also, was of course unknown to her primary self, but her subliminal self, in addition to its own private and constant stock of knowledge and opinions, had the advantage of more subtle means of securing other knowledge necessary for a proper answer, and so sought it in her husband's mind, or wherever it could be obtained. The sources of information accessible to the subliminal self, through means analogous to those which have been named—thought-transference and telepathy—are certainly various, and their limit is not yet known. We may mention, however, in this connection, besides the mind of the automatic writer—the mind of the questioner, and also the minds of other persons present, in any or all of which may be stored up knowledge or impressions of which the ordinary consciousness or memory retains no trace; it may be a scene witnessed in childhood; a newspaper paragraph read many years ago; a casual remark overheard, but not even noticed—all these and many more are sources of information upon which the subliminal self may draw for answers, which, when written out by the automatist, seem absolutely marvellous, not to say miraculous or supernatural.

Thus, the prayer at the ceremony of the advancement of a Mark Master Mason, although language entirely unfamiliar to Mrs. Newnham, was perfectly familiar to her husband, who was himself a Mason, and, I believe, a chaplain in the order; and while the form was not one actually used, it contained strictly accurate technicalities, and would have been perfectly appropriate to such an occasion.

The messages written by Mr. Wedgwood and Mrs. R. profess to come directly from the spirit of Colonel Gurwood; but without absolutely discarding that theory, having the key to which I have referred, let us see if such a supposition is necessary to explain the facts.

It may be conceded at once that neither Mr. Wedgwood nor either of the ladies with whom he wrote had any conscious knowledge of Col. Gurwood—his military career, or his sad taking off; but they were all intelligent people. John Gurwood, as it turned out, was a noted man; he was an officer in the Peninsular War, under the Duke of Wellington, performed an act of special bravery and daring, in the performance of which he was severely wounded, and for which he was afterward granted a coat of arms. He was also afterward chosen to edit the duke's dispatches. All this was recorded in the *Annual Register* for 1845, soon after Gurwood's death, together with a description in the language of heraldry of the crest or coat of arms which had been granted him many years before.

It is scarcely possible that such an event would

not have been noticed in the newspapers at the time of Gurwood's death, and nothing is more probable than that some of these intelligent persons had read these accounts, or as children heard them read or referred to, though they may now have been entirely absent from their ordinary consciousness and memory. At all events, the subliminal self or secondary consciousness of Mrs. R., whom Planchette designates as "the medium," or of Mr. Wedgwood, may have come into relationship with the sources of information necessary to furnish the messages which it communicated, and these sources may have been the knowledge or impressions unconsciously received many years before by some of those present, the generally diffused knowledge of these facts which doubtless prevailed in the community at the time of Gurwood's death, and the full printed accounts of these events, many copies of which were extant.

From the description of Gurwood's coat of arms the idea could easily have been obtained which Planchette rudely represented in drawing, constituting what is called a test, and also the other knowledge concerning his military career and death which appeared in the various messages.

Regarding cases coming under my own observation, the incident relating to Peter Stuyvesant's pear tree was well known to us both, and had only recently been a matter of general conversation, and all of those present had a more or less distinct idea of Peter Stuyvesant himself, derived from Irving's "Knickerbocker's History of New York."

Of the cases observed with Miss V., as before stated, nearly all the names given of "authorities," as we called them, were evidently fictitious, scarcely one being recognized, and none were of persons with whom we had any connection, and some did not claim any other origin than our subliminal consciousness, as was also the case with messages written by Mrs. Newnham.

If, then, some of the messages are surely the work of the subliminal self of the writer, aided by its more acute and more far-reaching perceptions, and if nearly all may be accounted for in the same way, the probability that all such messages have the same origin is greatly increased, and in the same degree the necessity for the spiritualistic theory is diminished, since it is evident that of two theories for explaining a new fact we should accept that one which better harmonizes with facts already established.

CHAPTER VIII.

AUTOMATIC WRITING, DRAWING AND PAINTING.

The subject of Automatism has thus far been illustrated by reference to Planchette-writing alone. It was selected because it is the kind most frequently seen and most easily proved by experiment. The little instrument Planchette, however, is not essential; it is used because, being placed on casters, it is more easily moved.

The Chinese, long ago, used for the same purpose a little basket, with style attached, placed upon two even chopsticks.

The same results also occur with some persons when the pencil is simply held in the usual manner for writing. The hand then being allowed to remain perfectly passive, automatic movements first take place—the hand moving round and round or across the paper, and then follows writing or drawing, as the case may be. Some persons produce written messages in *mirror writing* —that is, reversed—or so written that it can only be easily read by causing it to be reflected in a mirror. This kind of writing is sometimes produced on the first attempt of the experimenter, and even by young children without any experience or knowledge of the subject.

As previously shown, different strata of consciousness may, and in some well observed cases, most certainly do, exist in the same individual. In these well observed cases, each separate consciousness had its own distinct chain of memories and its own characteristics and peculiarities; and these distinct chains of memories and well defined characteristics constitute, so far as we can judge, distinct personalities. At all events, they are centres of intelligence and mental activity which are altogether independent of the ordinary, everyday consciousness or personality, and often altogether superior to it. Accordingly this other centre of intelligence and mental activity has been named the *second personality* or *subliminal self;* that is, a consciousness or self or personality beneath the threshold, so to speak, of the ordinary or primary self.

Ansel Bourne and A. J. Brown were separate and distinct personalities, having entirely distinct, and apparently unrelated, chains of memory, distinct characteristics, opinions, and peculiarities, acting at different times through the same body.

Ansel Bourne was the usual or primary personality; A. J. Brown was a second personality, a separate focus of intelligence and mental activity, a subliminal self. What the exact relationship existing between these two personalities may be we do not attempt at present to explain; but that they exist and act independent of each other we know. In other instances, as, for example, that of Madame B., the hypnotic subject of Prof. Janet of Havre, and also that of Alma Z., we have been able to observe these separate centres of intelligence, these distinct personalities, both in action at the same time, upon altogether separate and unrelated subjects. Sometimes the subliminal self takes full control, making itself the active ruling personality to the entire exclusion of the primary self; and sometimes it only sends messages to the primary or ordinary self, by suggestion, mental pictures, or vivid impressions made upon the organs of sense and producing the sensation of seeing, hearing, or touch.

To illustrate these different methods of communication between the ordinary and subliminal self, suppose an individual, whom we will designate as X., manifests this peculiar condition of double consciousness. As we have seen, the subliminal self often takes cognizance of things concerning which the ordinary self is entirely ignorant, but it may not always have the power to impress the primary self with this knowledge, nor to take full possession, so as to be able to impart it to others by speaking or writing. This is the usual condition of most persons; with some peculiarly constituted persons, however, the possibility of being so impressed surely exists, and with them these impressions are direct and vivid.

Our individual, X., is one in whom this ability to receive impressions in this manner exists.

To illustrate: Suppose first that X. is asleep, is taking his after-dinner nap, and that children playing in his grounds have set fire to some straw in close proximity to buildings near by. No one notices the danger. X. is asleep, but his subliminal self is on the alert—like the second self of the somnambulist or subject in the hypnotic trance—it sees that unless checked there will be a destructive conflagration. It impresses upon X. a dream of fire so vivid that he wakes in alarm, discovers the mischief and averts the danger. Or suppose X. to be awake and sitting in his office in a distant part of the house, quite unconscious of anything unusual. All at once he becomes restless, unable to pursue his work; he is impelled to leave his desk, to go out, to walk in the direction of the fire, and thus become aware of the danger. Or again, that X. is an automatic writer—that paper and pencil are at hand and he receives a sudden impulse to write. He has no knowledge of what he is writing, but upon examination he finds it a warning to look after the threatening fire; or still again, that he hears a voice distinctly saying, "Look out for fire;" or sees a distinct picture of the place and circumstances of the fire; all these are possible methods by which the subliminal self might communicate to X., the ordinary personality, the danger which was threatening.

Automatism, therefore, does not necessarily take the form of written messages, but may take any form by which the subliminal self can best transmit its message to the primary self—or in the same way from one person to another, whether by words written or spoken automatically—by voices heard, by action influenced, as when X. is influenced to leave his office and walk, or the mischievous Léontine unties the apron of Léonie, or by vision or vivid mental picture, as when Peter sees a "sheet let down by the four corners," from which he learns an important lesson.

The messages received automatically may not all be true; they may be trivial and even false; on the other hand, they may not only be true and important but they may convey information quite out of the power of the primary self to acquire by any ordinary use of the senses. Nor need we be greatly surprised at this; it is a normal function of the subliminal self; with some persons that function is active, with others it is dormant, but in all, at some moment in life, circumstances may arise which shall awaken that function into activity.

A remarkable example of messages received by automatic writing is that furnished by Mr. W. T. Stead, occurring in his own experience. Mr. Stead is a well-known author, journalist, and the editor of the London edition of the *Review of Reviews*, in which magazine his experiences have, on various occasions, been published.

As he regards the matter, there is an *invisible intelligence* which controls his hand, but the persons with whom he is in communication are alive and visible—for instance his own son on various occasions, also persons in his employ, writers upon his magazine, casual acquaintances, and even strangers.

None of these persons participate in any active or conscious way in the communications. Mr. F. W. H. Myers has often conversed with Mr. Stead and with several of his involuntary correspondents in relation to the phenomena, and the facts are so simple and open, and the persons connected with them so intelligent and evidently sincere and truthful, that no doubt can be entertained as to the reality of the incidents, however they may be interpreted.

One of the most remarkable of these involuntary correspondents is known as Miss A., a lady employed by him in literary work of an important character. She testifies in regard to the matter: "I, the subject of Mr. Stead's automatic writing, known as 'A.,' testify to the correctness of the statements made in this report. I would like to add what I think more wonderful than many things Mr. Stead has cited, namely, the correctness with which, on several occasions, he has given the names of persons whom he has never seen nor heard of before. I remember on one occasion a person calling upon me with a very uncommon name. The next day I saw Mr. Stead and he read to me what his hand had written of the visit of that person, giving the name absolutely correctly. Mr. Stead has never seen that person, and until then had no knowledge of his existence."

The following is a description of a journey made by Miss A., automatically written by Mr. Stead, he at the time not having the slightest knowledge where she was, what she was doing, or that she intended making any such journey. The slight inaccuracies are noted :—

" I went to the Waterloo station by the twelve o'clock train, and got to Hampton Court about one. When we got out we went to a hotel and had dinner. It cost nearly three shillings. After dinner I went to the picture-galleries. I was very much pleased with the paintings of many of the ceilings. I was interested in most of the portraits of Lely. After seeing the galleries I went into the grounds. How beautiful they are! I saw a great vine, that lovely English garden' the avenue of elms, the canal, the great water sheet, the three views, the fountain, the gold fishes, and then lost myself in the maze. I got home about nine o'clock. It cost me altogether about six shillings." On communicating this to Miss A. she found that everything was correct with two exceptions. She went down by the two o'clock train instead of the twelve, and got to Hampton Court about three. The dinner cost her two and elevenpence, which was nearly three shillings, and the total was six and threepence. The places were visited in the order mentioned.

A second instance was where the needs of a comparative stranger were written out by Mr. Stead's hand. Mr. Stead goes on to say: " Last February I met a correspondent in a railway carriage with whom I had a very casual acquaintance. Knowing that he was in considerable distress, our conversation fell into a more or less confidential train in which I divined that his difficulty was chiefly financial. I said I did not know whether I could be of any help to him, but asked him to let me know exactly how things stood—what were his debts, his expectations, and so forth. He said he really could not tell me, and I refrained from pressing him.

" That night I received a letter from him apologizing for not having given the information, but saying he really could not. I received that letter about ten o'clock, and about two o'clock next morning, before going to sleep, I sat down in my bedroom and said: 'You did not like to tell me your exact financial condition face to face, but now you can do so through my hand. Just write and tell me exactly how things stand. How much money do you owe?' My hand wrote,

'My debts are £90.' In answer to a further inquiry whether the figures were accurately stated, 'ninety pounds' was then written in full. 'Is that all?' I asked. My hand wrote 'Yes, and how I am to pay I do not know.' 'Well,' I said; 'how much do you want for that piece of property you wish to sell?' My hand wrote, 'What I hope is, say, £100 for that. It seems a great deal, but I must get money somehow. Oh, if I could get anything to do—I would gladly do anything!' 'What does it cost you to live?' I asked. My hand wrote, 'I do not think I could possibly live under £200 a year. If I were alone I could live on £50 per annum.'

"The next day I made a point of seeking my friend. He said: 'I hope you were not offended at my refusing to tell you my circumstances, but really I do not think it would be right to trouble you with them.' I said: 'I am not offended in the least, and I hope you will not be offended when I tell you what I have done.' I then explained this automatic, telepathic method of communication. I said: 'I do not know whether there is a word of truth in what my hand has written. I hesitate at telling you, for I confess I think the sum which was written as the amount of your debts cannot be correctly stated; it seems to me much too small, considering the distress in which you seemed to be; therefore I will read you that first, and if that is right I will read you the rest; but if it is wrong I will consider it is rubbish and that your mind in no way influenced my hand.' He was interested but incredulous. But, I said, 'Before I read you anything will you form a definite idea in your mind as to how much your debts amount to; secondly, as to the amount of money you hope to get for that property; thirdly, what it costs you to keep up your establishment with your relatives; and fourthly, what you could live upon if you were by yourself?' 'Yes,' he said, 'I have thought of all those things.' I then read out. 'The amount of your debts is about £90.' He started. 'Yes,' he said, 'that is right.' Then I said: 'As that is right I will read the rest. You hope to get £100 for your property.' 'Yes,' he said, 'that was the figure that was in my mind, though I hesitated to mention it for it seems too much.' 'You say you cannot live upon less than £200 a year with your present establishment.' 'Yes,' he said, 'that is exactly right.' 'But if you were by yourself you could live on £50 a year.' 'Well,' said he, 'a pound a week was what I had fixed in my mind.' Therefore there had been a perfectly accurate transcription of the thoughts in the mind of a comparative stranger written out with my own hand at a time when we were at a distance of some miles apart, within a few hours of the time when he had written apologizing for not having given me the information for which I had asked."

In the following case the correspondent is a foreign lady, doing some work for the *Review*, but whom Mr. Stead had only met once in his life. On the occasion now referred to he was to meet her at Redcar Station at about three o'clock in the afternoon. He was stopping at a house ten minutes' walk from the station, and it occurred to him that "about three o'clock," as mentioned in her letter, might mean *before* three; and it was now only twenty minutes of three. No timetable was at hand: he simply asked her to use his hand to tell him what time the train was due. This was done without ever having had any communication with her upon the subject of automatic writing. She (by Mr. Stead's hand) immediately wrote her name, and said the train was due at Redcar Station at ten minutes of three. Accordingly he had to leave at once—but before starting he said, "Where are you at this moment?" The answer came, "I am in the train at Middlesborough railway station, on my way from Hartpool to Redcar."

On arriving at the station he consulted the time-table and found the train was due at 2:52. The train, however, was late. At three o'clock it had not arrived; at five minutes past three, getting uneasy at the delay, he took paper and pencil in his hand and asked where she was.

Her name was at once written and there was added: "I am in the train rounding the curve before you come to Redcar Station—I will be with you in a minute."

"Why the mischief have you been so late?" he mentally asked. His hand wrote, "We were detained at Middlesborough so long—I don't know why."

He put the paper in his pocket and walked to the end of the platform just as the train came in.

He immediately went to his friend and exclaimed:—"How late you are! What on earth has been the matter?" To which she replied: "I do not know; the train stopped so long at Middlesborough—it seemed as if it never would start."

This narrative was fully corroborated by the lady who was the passenger referred to.

In all these cases it should be noticed the so-called correspondent took no active part in the experiment, was not conscious of communicating anything, nor of trying to do so; nor is there any evidence of a third party or any intervening intelligence or personality; but the subliminal self of the writer went forth and acquired the needed information and transferred it automatically to the primary self, as was the case in the Planchette-writing of Mrs. Newnham and the Wedgwood cases.

During the years 1874 and 1875 I had under my care Mrs. Juliette T. Burton, the wife of a physician who came to New York from the South at the close of the war. She was a woman of refinement, education, and excellent literary ability. She wrote with unusual facility, and her articles were accepted by newspapers and magazines, and brought her a considerable income. I knew her well, and her honesty, good faith, and strong common-sense were conspicuous. She died of phthisis in 1875. It is to her varied automatic powers as illustrating our subject that I would call attention.

Many of her best articles were prepared without conscious effort of her own, either physical or mental; she simply prepared pencils and paper, became passive, and her hand wrote. Sometimes she had a plan to write up a certain subject, and sometimes the subject as well as the matter came automatically.

She knew that she was writing, but of what was written she had no knowledge until she read her own manuscript.

She had no talent for drawing nor for painting; she could not, in her ordinary condition, draw a face, nor even a leaf, which could be recognized. Soon after coming to New York she began to see faces and other pictures before her on the blank paper and to sketch them with marvellous rapidity and exactness, all in the same automatic manner as that in which she did her writing. These drawings were not crude, but were strongly characteristic and were delicately done with ordinary lead pencils, several of which were prepared beforehand with sharp delicate points. I remember one drawing in particular—a man's head about half life-size, with full flowing beard. At first glance there was nothing peculiar about the picture, except that one would say that it was a strong and characteristic face; but on close examination in a strong light, and especially through a reading-glass, the beard was seen to be made up entirely of exceedingly minute faces of sheep;

every face was perfectly formed and characteristic, and there were thousands of them. It was done with the same wonderful rapidity which characterized all her automatic work.

Later she was impelled to procure colors, brushes, and all the materials for painting in oil; and although she had never even seen that kind of work done, and had not the slightest idea how to mix the colors to produce desired tints, nor how to apply them to produce desired effects, yet at a single sitting in a darkened room she produced a head of singular strength and character and possessing at least some artistic merit. Certainly no one could imagine it to be the first attempt of a person entirely without natural talent for either drawing or painting. It was done on common brown cardboard, and it has been in my possession for the past twenty-two years. The reproduction which appears as frontispiece to the present volume gives some idea of its character.

The impression received by the painter was that it was the portrait of an Englishman named Nathan Early.* No date was assigned.

As a further illustration of her automatic power, it may be mentioned that another uncultivated faculty developed itself, namely, the power of

* See Frontispiece.

referring to past events in the lives of those who were in her presence. The knowledge of past events so conveyed was frequently most remarkable and was circumstantially correct, even rivalling in this respect the reports which we have of Jung-Stilling and Zschokke.

CHAPTER IX.

CRYSTAL-GAZING.

AUTOMATIC messages fall naturally into two general classes: (1) *Motor* messages, or those received by means of writing, speaking, drawing, or some *activity* of the body, and (2) *sensory* messages, or those received *passively* by means of an impression made upon some of the senses, as, for example, seeing, hearing, or feeling.

The motor messages spelt out by raps and table-tipping, and the performances of trance-speakers and spiritualistic mediums need not detain us at present, so far as the messages themselves are concerned they offer no new elements for consideration. The utterances of trance-speakers as a rule are not rich in verifiable facts, though some of their performances are truly remarkable as presenting a phase of improvisation automatically given; and the same may be said of mediumistic utterances generally; they have the same value as automatic writing, whether produced by Planchette, or passively holding the pencil in the hand; and so far as they are honest they probably have the same origin, namely, the secondary consciousness or subliminal self of the medium. As regards the force which makes the raps or tips the table, it is altogether a different subject and its consideration here would be unnecessary and out of place.

I hasten to present cases of automatism where the messages brought are given by other means than writing, speaking, or any movement or activity of the body, but which belong to the *sensory* class, and are received by impressions made upon the senses. Of these the most common are those made upon the sense of sight.

To this class belong visions, dreams, distinct mental pictures presented under widely varying circumstances and conditions, in trance, in the hypnotic condition, in sleep, or directly conveyed to the primary conscious self. To simply *think* how a person, a building, or a landscape looks is one thing, but to have a full mental picture, possessing dimensions, and a stability which admits of being closely examined in detail, is quite another thing.

A little girl of my acquaintance, on returning from the country after several weeks of absence from her father, said to him,—"Why, papa, I could have you with me whenever I liked, this summer, though it was only your head and shoulders that I could see; but I could place you where I liked and could look at you a long time before you went away." Without knowing it the child exactly described a true vision—her thought of her father was visualized, *externalized*, given a form which had definiteness, which could be placed and examined in detail, and was more or less permanent.

Various artificial expedients have been resorted to in order to assist in this process of distinct visualization; and of these artificial means one of the most important and effective is known as crystal-gazing.

It is a fact not often commented upon—indeed not often alluded to in general literature—that the crystal has from the earliest times been made use of for the purpose of producing visions, and for divination and prophecy. Not only has the crystal been used for this purpose, but also the mirror, a cup or glass of water or wine, or even some dark and glistening substance like treacle or ink poured into the palm of the hand, have all been used in a similar manner. The same practice is still observed amongst the people of India as his breast. Mr. Lane adds, "Without saying that I suspected the boy had made a mistake I asked the magician whether objects appeared in the ink as if actually before the boy's eyes, or as if in a glass, which made the right side appear the left? He replied, 'They appear as in a mirror.' This rendered the boy's description faultless."

It is remarkable to notice how prevalent this mode of divination or second-sight has been in all ages. Traces of the same procedure have been found in Egypt, Persia, China, India, Greece, and Rome, and notably in Europe generally, from the tenth to the sixteenth centuries. A lady who withholds her name from the public, but who is perfectly well known to Mr. Myers, of the Society for Psychical Research, and who chooses to be known as Miss X., has been at great pains to collect curious information upon this subject and has added her own very interesting experience in crystal-gazing. She writes, "It is interesting to observe the close resemblance in the various methods of employing the mirror, and in the mystic symbolism which surrounds it, not only in different ages, but in different countries. From the time of the Assyrian monarch represented on the walls of the northwest palace of Nimrod down to the seventeenth century, when Dr. Dee placed his 'Shew Stone' on a cushioned table in the goodly little chapel next his chamber in the college of which he was warden at Manchester, the seer has surrounded himself with the ceremonials of worship, whether to propitiate Pan or Osiris, or to disconcert Ahriman or the Prince of Darkness."

The early Jewish Scriptures abound in indications of the same practice. When the patriarch Joseph put his silver cup in the mouth of his young brother Benjamin's sack, in order that he might have a pretext for recalling his brethren after he had sent them away, his steward, in accusing them of theft, uses this language: "Is not this the cup in which my lord drinketh, and *whereby indeed he divineth?*" Showing the same use of the cup for purposes of divination as that indicated on the walls of the Assyrian Palace.

The Urim and Thummim, as their names indicate, were doubtless stones of unusual splendor set in the high-priest's "breast-plate of judgment," and they were made use of to "inquire of the Lord."

When Joshua was to be set apart as a leader of the people, he was brought to Eleazar the priest, who should lay his hands on him and "ask counsel for him *after the judgment* of *Urim* before the Lord." In the last days of Saul's career as King of Israel he desired to "inquire of the Lord" regarding his future fortunes, but "the Lord answered him not, neither by dreams, nor by *Urim*, nor by prophets; and it is not uninteresting to note that Saul in his strait directly sought the Witch of Endor, from whom he obtained what proved to be true information regarding the disasters which were to overwhelm him.

In a Persian romance it is noted that "if a mirror be covered with ink and placed in front of any one it will indicate whatever he wishes to know."

The Greeks had a variety of methods of divination by crystal-gazing. Sometimes it was by the mirror placed so as to reflect light upon the surface of a fountain of clear water, sometimes by mirrors alone; sometimes they made use of glass vessels filled with water and surrounded with torches, sometimes of natural crystals, and sometimes even of a child's "nails covered with oil and soot," so as to reflect the rays of the sun.

The Romans made special use of crystals and mirrors, and children were particularly employed for mirror-reading when consulting regarding important events; thus in a manner taking the place of the early oracles. From Jewish and Pagan practices as a means of divination, clairvoyance and prophecy, the art of the crystal seer seems to have passed to early Christian times without material change except in ceremonials. These seers are mentioned in the counsels of the Church as specularii, children often acting as the seers, and although in some quarters they were looked upon with suspicion as heretics, and were under the ban of the Church, yet they had an extensive following.

Thomas Aquinas, speaking of the peculiar power of seeing visions possessed by children, says it is not to be ascribed to any virtue or innocence of theirs, nor any power of nature, but that it is the work of the devil.

In Wagner's beautiful opera of Parsifal, based upon the legend of the Holy Grail, reference to the same custom is more than once evident. The second act opens with a scene representing the enchanted castle of Klingsor; the magician himself is seen gazing into a bright metallic mirror, in which he sees Parsifal approaching and recognizes and fears him as the promised guiltless one —the true king and guardian of the Grail—an office to which he himself had once aspired. In fact the Grail itself, in its earliest mythical and traditional form, as well as in its later development as a distinctly Christian symbol, was an instrument of divination and prophecy. The Druids had their basin, sometimes filled with aromatic herbs, sometimes with the blood of the sacrificed victim; but in either case it was potent for securing the proper psychic condition in the officiating priest or soothsayer; and while Arabic and Indian myths present the same idea, sometimes as a cup of divination, and sometimes as a brilliant stone, the British Islands were the main source of the traditions which eventually culminated in the legends of the Holy Grail, with its full store of beautiful and touching incidents, prophecies, and forms of worship. In each the special guardians and knights of the Grail appear, with Parsifal, the simple-minded, pure and pitiful knight as its restorer and king when lost or in unworthy hands.

In the German version of the twelfth century as given by Wolfram, in his Parzival, the Grail is a beautiful, sacred stone, enshrined in the magnificent temple at Montsalvat, guarded by the consecrated knights and the sick and erring, but repentant, King Amfortas. While the unhappy king was worshipping with gaze intent upon the Sacred Emblem, suddenly letters of fire surrounded it and he read the cheering prophecy:

> "In the loving soul of a guiltless one
> Put thy faith—Him have I chosen."

Kufferath remarks, "The religious emblem soon became a symbolic object—it revealed to its worshippers the knowledge of the future, the mystery of the world, the treasures of human knowledge, and imparted a poetic inspiration." So it comes to pass that in the legend in its latest form—the splendid work of the Master of Bayreuth, the Holy Grail, as a chalice and Christian emblem, is still endowed with the same miraculous power, and is rescued from the unfortunate guardianship of Amfortas by the "loving soul of a guiltless one"—the simple, tried, and much-enduring Parsifal, miraculously promised long before by the Grail itself.

It will be seen, then, that crystal-gazing in its various forms has, from the earliest times, been practised with great ceremony for the purpose of acquiring knowledge concerning affairs and events unknown and often not discoverable by ordinary methods.

Stripped of its fictitious accessories—its charms, incantations, incense and prayers—one single important fact remains common in the most ancient and the most modern usages, and that fact is the steady and continuous gazing at a bright object. It is identical with Braid's method of inducing the hypnotic trance, with Luys' method, causing his patients to gaze at revolving mirrors, and with the method of hypnotizers generally who desire their patients to direct their gaze toward some specified, and preferably some bright or reflecting object.

In crystal-gazing, as ordinarily practised, the full hypnotic condition is not usually induced; but in many cases a condition of reverie occurs, in which pictures or visions fill the mind or appear externalized in the crystal or mirror. With some persons this condition so favorable to visualizing, is produced by simply becoming passive; with others the gazing at a bright or reflecting object assists in securing that end, while with many none of these means, nor yet the assistance of the most skilful hypnotizer, avails to secure the message-bearing action of the subliminal self.

The experiences of Miss X., in crystal-gazing are devoid of the interest imparted by exciting incident, and on that very account are the more valuable as illustrating our subject. She has friends of whose experiments she has carefully observed the results, and she has some seventy cases or experiments of her own of which she has kept carefully prepared notes, always made directly or within an hour after each experiment. For a crystal she recommends "a good-sized magnifying glass placed on a dark background."

She classifies her results as follows:—

(1) After-images or recrudescent memories coming up from the subconscious strata to which the had fallen.

(2) Objectivations, or the visualizing of ideas or images which already exist consciously or unconsciously in the mind.

(3) Visions possibly telepathic, or clairvoyant, implying acquirement of knowledge by supranormal means.

The following are some of Miss X.'s experiments:—

She had been occupying herself with accounts and opened a drawer to take out her banking book; accidentally her hand came in contact with the crystal she was in the habit of using, and she welcomes the suggestion of a change of occupation. Figures, however, were still uppermost, and the crystal showed her nothing but the combination 7694. Dismissing this as probably the number of the cab she had driven in that morning, or a chance combination of figures with which she had been occupied, she laid aside the crystal and took up her banking book, which certainly she had not seen for several months. Greatly to her surprise she found that 7694 was the number of her book, plainly indicated on the cover.

She declares that she would have utterly failed to recall the figures, and could not even have guessed the number of digits nor the value of the first figure.

Again:—Having carelessly destroyed a letter without preserving the address of her correspondent she tried in vain to recall it. She knew the county, and, searching on a map, she recognized the name of the town, one quite unfamiliar to her, but she had no clue to the house or street, till at length it occurred to her to test the value of the crystal as a means of recalling forgotten knowledge. A short inspection showed her the words, "H. House," in gray letters on a white ground. Having nothing better to rely upon she risked posting the letter to the address so curiously supplied. A day or two brought an answer—on paper headed "H. House" in gray letters on a white ground.

One more illustration from Miss X., one of her earliest experiments, numbered 11, in her note-book. There came into the crystal a vision perplexing and wholly unexpected: a quaint old chair, an aged hand, a worn black coat-sleeve resting on the arm of the chair. It was slowly recognized as a recollection of a room in a country vicarage which she had not been in and had seldom thought of since she was a child of ten. But whence came the vision, and why to-day? The clue was found. That same day she had been reading Dante, a book which she had first learned to read and enjoy by the help of the aged vicar with the "worn black coat-sleeve" resting on the same quaint, oak chair-arm in that same corner of the study in the country vicarage.

Here are two cases from the same writer belonging to the third division of her classification, namely, where an explanation of the vision requires the introduction of a telepathic influence. On Monday, February 11th, she took up the crystal with the deliberate wish and intention of seeing a certain figure which occupied her thoughts at the time; but instead of the desired figure the field was preoccupied by a plain little nosegay of daffodils, such as might be formed by two or three fine flowers bunched together.

This presented itself in several different positions notwithstanding her wish to be rid of it, so as to have the field clear for her desired picture. She concluded that the vision came in consequence of her having the day before seen the first daffodils of the season on a friend's dinner-table. But the resemblance to these was not at all complete, as they were loosely arranged with ferns and ivy, whereas the crystal vision was a compact little bunch without foliage of any kind. On Thursday, February 14th, she very unexpectedly received as a "Valentine" a painting on a blue satin ground, of a bunch of daffodils corresponding exactly with her crystal vision. She also ascertained that on Monday the 11th, the artist had spent several hours in making studies of these flowers, arranged in different positions.

Again:—On Saturday, March 9th, she had written a rather impatient note to a friend, accusing her of having, on her return from the Continent, spent several days in London without visiting her. On Sunday evening following, she found her friend before her in the crystal, but could not understand why she held up in a deprecating manner what seemed to be a music portfolio. However, she made a note of the vision and sketched the portfolio. On Monday she received an answer to her impatient letter, pleading guilty to the charge of neglect, but urging as an excuse that she was attending the Royal Academy of Music and was engaged there the greater part of every day. Such an excuse was to the last degree unexpected, as her friend was a married woman and had never given serious attention to music. It was true, however—and she afterwards learned that she carried a portfolio which was the counterpart of the one she had sketched from her crystal vision.

The following incident in which an East India army officer, Col. Wickham, his wife, Princess di Cristoforo, and Ruth, their educated native servant, were the chief actors, illustrates another phase of crystal-gazing. All three of the actors participating in the incident were well known personally to Mr. Myers, who reports the case. Briefly stated: In 1885, Colonel, then Major, Wickham, was stationed with the Royal Artillery at Colabra, about two miles from Bombay. Mrs. Wickham was accustomed to experiment with some of the Indian servants and especially Ruth, by having her look in a glass of magnetized water. One morning Lord Reay was expected to arrive at Bombay, and there was to be a grand full-dress parade of the English troops. While sitting at the breakfast table the major directed his orderly to see that his uniform was in readiness. The man obeyed, but soon returned with a dejected air, and stammered out—"Sahib, me no can find the dress pouch-belt." A general hunt for the lost article was instituted, but to no purpose; the pouch-belt was absolutely missing. The enraged major stormed and accused the servants of stealing it, which only produced a tumult and a storm of denials from them all. "Now," cried the major, "is an excellent opportunity to test the seeing powers of Ruth. Bring her in at once and let her try if she can find my pouch-belt." Accordingly a tumbler was filled with water, and Mrs. W. placing it on her left hand made passes over it with her right. Water so treated could always be detected with absolute certainty by Ruth, simply by tasting it—a fact not uncommonly observed, and which was an additional proof that she possessed unusual perceptive power. Into this glass of water Ruth gazed intently, but she could discern nothing. She was commanded to find the thief, but no thief could be seen. Changing her tactics, Mrs. W. then commanded Ruth to see where the major was the last time he wore the belt. At once she described the scene of a grand parade which took place months before, and which they all recognized. "Do not take your eyes off from the major for a moment," said Mrs. W., and Ruth continued to gaze intently at the pageant in the glass. At length the parade ended and Ruth said, "Sahib has gone into a big house by the water; all his regimentals are put in the tin case, but the pouch-belt is left out; it is hanging on a peg in the dressing-room of the big house by the water." "The yacht club!" cried the major. "Patilla, send some one at once to see if the belt has been left there." The search was rewarded by finding the belt as described, and the servants returned bringing it with a grand tumult of triumph. On many other occasions was Ruth's aid successfully invoked to find lost articles.

Instead of a glass of water, some springs and wells when gazed into have the same effect of producing visions, especially when a mirror is so held at the same time as to reflect light upon the surface of the water. Springs of this sort have been reported at various periods in the past, some being frequented for health and some for purposes of divination. The latest instance of a well possessing the quality or power of producing visions is that upon the farm of Col. J. J. Deyer at Handsoms, Va. It was in May, 1892, that the curious influence pertaining to this well was first observed and soon it was thronged with visitors. Faces, both familiar and strange, of people living and of those long dead, and hundreds of other objects, animate and inanimate, were distinctly seen upon the surface of the water. The water of the well is *unusually clear* and the bottom of *white sand* is clearly visible. A mirror is held over the top of the well with face toward the water so as to throw reflected light upon the surface. At first Miss Deyer, the colonel's daughter, always held the mirror, but afterwards it was found that any one who could hold the mirror *steadily* performed the duty equally well. If the mirror was held unsteadily the pictures were indistinct or failed to appear at all; and the brighter the day the better the pictures. Many level headed men and some well qualified to observe curious psychical phenomena visited the well, and nearly all were convinced that, under favorable circumstances, remarkable pictures appeared; naturally, however, different causes were assigned for these appearances. Prof. Dolbear and Mr. T. E. Allen, from the American Psychical Society, saw nothing remarkable during their visit to the well, and referred the pictures seen by so many people to the reflection of objects about the well, aided by the mental excitement and expectation of so many spectators. This explanation, however, seems hardly sufficient to account for the hallucinations of so large a number of persons kept up for so long a time. At all events, an interesting psychic element of some sort was active.

Col. Deyer is an intelligent man, commanding the respect of his neighbors, and has held an appointment of considerable importance under the government at Washington. In a letter dated December 2d, 1893, he says :—" Thousands of people from various sections of the Union have visited the place—of course some laugh at it. I do myself sometimes, as I am not superstitious and take little stock in spooks or anything connected therewith ; but the well is here, and still shows up many wondrous things, but not so plentiful nor so plainly as it did a year ago."

We have presented in this well the most favorable conditions possible for crystal-gazing—a body of unusually clear sparkling water, lying upon a white sand bottom, and the rays of the sun reflected into it by means of a mirror ;—no better " cup of divination " could be desired, nor any better circumstances for securing the psychical conditions favorable for the action of the subliminal self.

The various methods of practising crystal-gazing here noticed may be looked upon simply as so many different forms of *sensory automatism*, referable in these instances to the sense of sight; and whether produced by using the "cup of divination," the ink or treacle in the palm of the hand, the jewels of the Jewish high-priest, the ordinary crystal or stone of the early Christian centuries, and even down to the experiments of Miss X., and the Society for Psychical Research, or last of all, the wells or springs of clear water, either the early ones of Greece and Rome, or the latest one on the farm of Col. Deyer, they are all simply methods of securing such a condition by gazing fixedly at a bright object, as best to facilitate communication between the ordinary or primary self, and the secondary or subliminal self. It is the first, and perhaps the most important, in a series of sensory automatisms, or those having reference to the senses, in distinction from motor automatisms, or those produced by various automatic actions of the body.

These sensory automatisms are usually looked upon as hallucinations—but so far as the term hallucination conveys the idea of deception or falsity it is inappropriate, since the messages brought in this manner are just as real—just as veridical or truth-telling as automatic writing or speaking.

Hearing is another form of sensory automatism, which, while less common than that of seeing, has also been noticed in all ages.

The child Samuel, ministering to the High Priest Eli, three times in one night, heard himself called by name, and three times came to Eli saying, "Here am I;" adding at last, "for surely thou didst call me." The wise high-priest recognized the rare psychic qualities of the child and brought him up for the priesthood in place of his own wayward sons; and he became the great seer of Israel.

Socrates was accustomed to hear a voice which always admonished him when the course he was pursuing or contemplating was wrong or harmful; but it was silent when the contemplated course was right. This was the famous "Dæmon of Socrates," and was described and discussed by Xenophon and Plato as well as other Greek writers and many modern ones. Socrates himself called it the "Divine Sign." And on that account he was accused of introducing new gods, and thus offering indignity to the accredited gods of Greece. On this, as one of the leading charges, Socrates was tried and condemned to death; but in all the proceedings connected with his trial and condemnation he persisted in his course which he knew would end in his death, rather than be false to his convictions of duty and right; and this he did because the voice—the " Divine Sign "—which always before had restrained him in any wrong course, was not heard restraining him in his present course.

Only once was it heard, and that was to restrain him from preparing any set argument in his defence before his judges. So he accepted his sentence and drank the hemlock, surrounded by his friends, to whom he calmly explained that death could not be an evil thing, not only from the arguments which he had adduced, but also because the Divine Sign, which never failed to admonish him when pursuing any harmful course, had not admonished nor restrained him in this course which had led directly to his death.

Joan of Arc heard voices, which in childhood only guided her in her ordinary duties, but which in her early womanhood made her one of the most conspicuous figures in the history of her time. They placed her, a young and unknown peasant girl, as a commander at the head of the defeated, disorganized, and discouraged armies of France, aroused them to enthusiasm, made them victorious, freed her country from the power of England, and placed the rightful prince upon the throne. She also heard and obeyed her guiding voices, even unto martyrdom.

Numerous instances might be cited occurring in ancient and also in modern times where the subliminal self has sent its message of instruction, guidance, warning, or restraint to the primary self by means of impressions made upon the organ of hearing. Socrates, Joan of Arc, Swedenborg, and many others considered these instructions infallible, supernatural, or divine; but in other cases the messages so given have been trivial, perhaps even false, thus removing the element of infallibility and absolute truthfulness from messages of this sort, and at the same time casting a doubt upon their supernatural character in any case. It seems wisest, therefore, at least to examine these and all cases of automatically received messages, whether by writing, trance-speaking, dreams, visions, or the hearing of voices, with a definite conception of a real and natural cause and origin for these messages in a subliminal self, forming a definite part of each individual: bearing in mind also that this subliminal self possesses powers and characteristics varying in each individual case, in many cases greatly transcending the powers and capabilities of the normal or primary self. But infallibility, though sometimes claimed, is by no means to be expected from this source, and the messages coming from each subliminal self must be judged and valued according to their own intrinsic character and merit, just as a message coming to us from any primary self, whether known or unknown to us, must be judged and valued according to its source, character, and merit.

CHAPTER X.

PHANTASMS.

PERHAPS no department of Psychical Research is looked upon from such divers and even quite opposite standpoints as that which relates to Apparitions or Phantasms. Many intelligent people, in a general way, accept them as realities but assign for them a supernatural origin; while others discredit them altogether because they have apparently no basis except an assumed supernatural one.

It has been said that primitive, undeveloped, and ignorant people almost universally believe in ghosts; while with the advance of civilization, culture, and general intelligence, the frequency of alleged apparitions and the belief in ghosts diminishes or altogether disappears. If this statement were to stand unqualified, by so much would the reality and respectability of phantasms be discredited. Possibly, however, it may be found that the last word has not yet been said, and that there may exist a scientific aspect for even so unstable and diaphanous a subject as ghosts.

Instead of going over the literature of the subject from the earliest times—a literature, by the way, which in the hands of Tylor, Maury, Scott, Ralston, Mrs. Crowe and others certainly does not lack interest—it will better suit our present purpose to examine some facts relative to perception in general and vision in particular, and give some examples illustrating different phases of the subject.

Perception may be defined as the cognizance which the mind takes of impressions presented to it through the organs of sense, and possibly also by other means.

One class of perceptions is universally recognized and is in a measure understood, namely, perceptions arising from impressions made by recognized external objects or forces upon the organs of sense, sight, hearing, smell, taste, and also the general sense of touch. These perceptions in particular are designated as *real* or *true*, because they correspond to recognized external realities.

But impressions are also made upon the organs of special sense by influences which are not recognized as having any objective reality, but which nevertheless affect the senses in a manner often identical with that in which they are affected by recognized external objects, and they cause the same perceptions to arise in the mind. Hence another broad class of perceptions includes those which are taken cognizance of by the mind from impressions made upon the organs of sense in other ways and by other means than by external objects, and often where there is no evidence that any external object exists corresponding to the impression so made. Perceptions arising in these various ways are called *hallucinations*.

On close examination, however, it is found that the sharp line of separation between what has and what has not an objective reality is not easily drawn, any more than in biology the sharp line between animal and vegetable life can be easily drawn, or at the lower end of the scale between the living and the not living.

So the origin of those perceptions which are classed as hallucinations has always been a subject of controversy, even among philosophers of the greatest merit and eminence.

Without following out the discussions which have arisen on this point—discussions which are often confusing and generally inconclusive, a fairly distinct view of the subject may be obtained by considering the origin of these perceptions under three heads—namely :—

(1) Perceptions which are reckoned as hallucinations may be originated *centrally;* that is, they may arise wholly within the mind itself without any direct external stimulus. For instance the characters drawn by the novelist may become so real to him, and even to some of his readers, that they become *externalized*—actual objects of visual perception and are seen to act and even heard to speak. The instance is repeatedly quoted of the painter who, after carefully studying a sitter's appearance, could voluntarily project it visibly into space and paint the portrait, not from the original, but from the phantasm so produced; and of another who could externalize and project other mental pictures in the same manner, pictures which so interested him and were so subject to the ordinary laws of vision that he would request any one who took a position in front of them, to move away so as not to obstruct his view.

It will be noticed in these cases that although the perception has its origin centrally, in the mind itself, and is even voluntarily produced, still, it is seen as an impression made upon the visual organ in exactly the same manner as a picture thrown upon the retina by a real external object; it disappears when the eyes are closed or an opaque object intervenes, and follows the laws of optics in general; hence, strictly speaking, these perceptions are also real.

(2) Perceptions may have their origin *peripherally*—that is, the point of excitation which causes the act of perception in the mind may exist in the external sense organs themselves, even when no external object corresponding to the perception exists at the time, or it is not in a position on account of distance or intervening objects to affect the senses.

In examining the cases which may be placed under this head they resolve themselves into two classes: those which occur in connection with some disease or defect in the sense organ concerned, and those which are recrudescences or after-visions, arising from over-excitation of those organs; for instance, after looking through a window in a very bright light—even a considerable length of time afterwards—on shutting the eyes or looking into a dark room, an image of the window is seen with all its divisions and peculiarities of construction distinctly presented. To the country lad returning home at night from his first visit to the circus the whole scene is again presented; and ring, horses, equestrians, acrobats and clowns are all seen and externalized with the utmost distinctness; even the crack of the ringmaster's whip is heard and the jokes and antics of the clowns repeated.

(3) Perceptions may have their origin telepathically—that is, scenes and incidents transpiring at a distance far too great to affect the bodily organs of sense in any direct or ordinary way do, nevertheless, in some way, cause perceptions to arise in the mind corresponding to those same scenes and incidents.

This is comparatively a new proposition in psychology and has for its basis studies and experiments which have only been systematically made within the past fourteen years. These studies and experiments relate to telepathy, automatism, and the action of the subliminal self. They have been undertaken and carried on by various societies interested in experimental psychology, but chiefly by the English Society for Psychical Research, some of the results of whose labors have been briefly sketched in the preceding chapters.

In addition to the reports of these societies an important contribution to the subject of apparitions was published by the then secretaries of the Society for Psychical Research, the late Mr. Edmund Gurney, Mr. Frederick W. H. Myers, and Mr. Frank Podmore.

It appeared under the title, *Phantasms of the Living*, and contained more than seven hundred instances relating to various forms of hallucinations and phantasms—carefully studied and authenticated cases which were selected from several thousand presented for examination. It is to these sources chiefly that I shall refer for cases illustrating the subject under consideration.

It seems hardly necessary to recapitulate here the experiments on which the doctrine of telepathy or thought-transference is established—experiments which have been carefully made by so many well qualified persons, and which have proved convincing to nearly every one, whether scientific or unscientific, who has patiently followed them, though of course not convincing to those who choose to remain ignorant of the facts.

The same is true regarding the subject of automatism and the existence and action of the subliminal self. It remains to show the interesting relations which these subjects bear to hallucinations in general, and especially to phantasms and apparitions.

INFLUENCED AT A DISTANCE.

It is well known that hallucinations can be voluntarily or purposely produced by one person in the mind of another, and in various ways, though few perhaps consider to what an extent this is possible. In many of the most astonishing feats of the conjurer, and especially of the Indian fakir, suggestion and the imagination are brought into service to aid in producing the illusions.

Regarding the hallucinations which may be produced in the mind of the hypnotized subject by the hypnotizer there can be no doubt.

The following case is in point and illustrates telepathic influence excited at a distance as well. It is from *Phantasms of the Living*, and the agent, Mr. E. M. Glissold, of 3 Oxford Square, W., writes substantially as follows: —

"In the year 1878 there was a carpenter named Gannaway employed by me to mend a gate in my garden; when a friend of mine (Moens) called upon me and the conversation turned upon mesmerism. He asked me if I knew anything about it myself. On my replying in the affirmative he said, 'Can you mesmerize any one at a distance?' I said that I had never tried to do so, but that there was a man in the garden whom I could easily mesmerize, and that I would try the experiment with this man if he (Moens) would tell me what to do. He then said, 'Form an impression of the man whom you wish to mesmerize, in your own mind, and then wish him strongly to come to you.'

"I very much doubted the success of the experiment, but I followed the directions of my friend, and I was extremely astonished to hear the steps of the man whom I wished to appear, running after me; he came up to me directly and asked me what I wanted with him. I will add that my friend and I had been walking in the garden and had seen and spoken with the carpenter, but when I wished him to come to me I was quite out of his sight behind the garden wall, one hundred yards distant, and had neither by conversation nor otherwise led him to believe that I intended to mesmerize him.

"On another occasion, when the Hon. Auberon Herbert was present, the following scene occurred. Gannaway was mesmerized and stood in one corner of the dining-room. Herbert sat at the table and wrote the following programme, each scene of which Mr. Glissold, the magnetizer, was to *silently call up in his own mind*.

"(1) I see a house in flames.

"(2) I see a woman looking out of a window.

"(3) She has a child in her arms.

"(4) She throws it out of the window.

"(5) Is it hurt—?

"Gannaway became much excited, describing each scene as it passed through the mind of his hypnotizer. Several well known persons add their testimony to the above statement."

A single case of mental action so strange and unusual, no matter how well authenticated, might not impress a cautious truth-seeker, but when fortified by well studied cases in the experience of such men as Esdaile, as shown in his remarkable experiments upon the natives of India, and especially his well known one of hypnotizing the blind man at a distance, also those of Prof. Janet, Prof. Richet, Dr. Gibert, and Dr. Héricourt, in France under the observation of Mr. Myers and other members of the Society for Psychical Research, and hundreds of other cases of hypnotizing at a distance, or silently influencing the subject without hypnotization, the matter then challenges attention and belief;—and it is from abundant observation of such cases, from the simplest examples of thought-transference to the most wonderful exhibition of perceptive power at great distances, that the doctrine of Telepathy is founded.

In the following case the agent was able to

project his own semblance or phantasm a distance of several miles; and it was then distinctly perceived by a young lady, a friend of the agent. The circumstances were these:—Two young men, Mr. A. H. W. Cleave and Mr. H. P. Sparks, aged respectively eighteen and nineteen years, were fellow-students of engineering at the Navy Yard, Portsmouth, England. While there, they engaged in some mesmeric experiments, and after a time Sparks was able to put Cleave thoroughly into the hypnotic condition. The following is Mr. Sparks' account of what occurred.

"For the last year or fifteen months I have been in the habit of mesmerizing a fellow-student of mine. The way I did it was by simply looking into his eyes as he lay in an easy position on a bed. This produced sleep. After a few times I found that this sleep was deepened by making long passes after the patient was off. Then comes the remarkable part of this sort of mesmerism." (Mr. Sparks then describes his subject's ability to see in his trance places in which he was interested if he resolved to see them before he was hypnotized.) "However, it has been during the last week or so I have been surprised and startled by an extraordinary affair. Last Friday evening (Jan. 15th, 1886), he (Cleave) expressed his wish to see a young lady living in Wandsworth, and he also said he would try to make himself seen by her. I accordingly mesmerized him and continued the long passes for about twenty minutes, concentrating my will on his idea. When he came round (after one hour and twenty minutes' trance) he said he had seen her in the dining-room; and that after a time she grew restless; then suddenly she looked straight at him, and then covered her eyes with her hands; just then he came round. Last Monday evening (Jan. 18th) we did the same thing, and this time he said he thought he had frightened her, as after she had looked at him a few minutes she fell back in her chair in a sort of faint. Her little brother was in the room at the time. Of course after this he expected a letter if the vision was real; and on Wednesday morning he received a letter from the young lady, asking whether anything had happened to him, as on Friday evening she was startled by seeing him standing at the door of the room. After a minute he disappeared and she thought it might have been fancy; but on Monday evening she was still more startled by seeing him again, and this time much clearer, and it so frightened her that she nearly fainted."

Mr. Cleave also writes a very interesting account of his experience in the matter, and two fellow-students who were in the room during the experiments also write corroborating the statements made.

The following is a copy of the letter in which the young lady, Miss A., describes her side of the affair. It is addressed, "Mr. A. H. W. Cleave, H. M. S. *Marlborough*, Portsmouth," and is postmarked Wandsworth, Jan. 19th, 1886.

"WANDSWORTH,
"Tuesday morning.

"DEAR ARTHUR,—Has anything happened to you? Please write and let me know at once, for I have been so frightened.

"Last Tuesday evening I was sitting in the dining-room reading, when I happened to look up, and could have declared I saw you standing at the door looking at me. I put my handkerchief to my eyes, and when I looked again you were gone.

"I thought it must have been only my fancy, but last night (Monday) while I was at supper I saw you again just as before, and was so frightened that I nearly fainted. Luckily only my brother was there or it would have attracted attention. Now do write at once and tell me how you are. I really cannot write any more now."

Probably the young lady is in error regarding the date of the first experiment, which may be accounted for by her excited condition—the shock of the last experiment having proved decidedly serious, as was afterwards discovered, and she begged that the experiment might never be repeated.

Both young men mention Friday as the day of their first decided success, but they were experimenting on previous days, including Tuesday, when the young lady writes she first saw Cleave's phantasm. Concerning the date of the last experiment there is no question.

Effects similar to those just related may also occur where the agent is in ordinary sleep, or at least when no hypnotizing process is made use of. The agent in this case first formulates the wish or strong resolution to be present and be seen at a certain place or by a certain person, and then goes to sleep, and generally remains unconscious of the result until learned from the percipient.

In the following case the name of the agent is withheld from publication, though known to Mr. Myers who reports the case; the percipient is the Rev. W. Stainton-Moses. The agent goes on to state :—

"One evening early last year (1878), I resolved to try to appear to Z. (Mr. Moses) at some miles distant. I did not inform him beforehand of my intended experiment, but retired to rest shortly before midnight with thoughts intently fixed on Z., with whose room and surroundings, however, I was quite unacquainted. I soon fell asleep and woke up the next morning unconscious of anything having taken place. On seeing Z. a few days afterwards I inquired, 'Did anything happen at your rooms on Saturday night?' 'Yes,' he replied, 'a great deal happened. I had been sitting over the fire with M., smoking and chatting. About 12:30 he rose to leave, and I let him out myself. I returned to the fire to finish my pipe when I saw you sitting in the chair just vacated by him. I looked intently at you, and then took up a newspaper to assure myself I was not dreaming, but on laying it down I saw you still there. While I gazed without speaking, you faded away. Though I imagined you must be fast asleep in bed at that hour, yet you appeared dressed in your ordinary garments, such as you usually wear every day.' 'Then my experiment seems to have succeeded,' I said. 'The next time I come ask me what I want, as I had fixed on my mind certain questions to ask you, but

I was probably waiting for an invitation to speak.'

"A few weeks later the experiment was repeated with equal success, I, as before, not informing Z. when it was made. On this occasion he not only questioned me upon the subject which was at that time under very warm discussion between us, but detained me by the exercise of his will, some time after I had intimated a desire to leave. As on the former occasion no recollection remained of the event, or seeming event, of the preceding night."

Mr. Moses writes, September 27th, 1885, confirming this account. Mr. Moses also says that he has never on any other occasion seen the figure of a living person in a place where the person was not.

The next case, while presenting features similar to the last, differs from it in this respect: that there are two percipients. It is copied from the manuscript book of the agent, Mr. S. H. B.

Mr. B. writes:—" On a certain Sunday evening in November, 1881, having been reading of the great power which the human will is capable of exercising, I determined with the whole force of my being that I would be present in spirit in the front bedroom, on the second floor of a house situated at 22 Hogarth Road, Kensington, in which room slept two ladies of my acquaintance, Miss L. S. V. and Miss E. C. V., aged respectively twenty-five and eleven years. I lived at this time at 23 Kildare Gardens, a distance of about three miles from Hogarth Road, and I had not mentioned in any way my intention of trying this experiment to either of the above named ladies, for the simple reason that it was only on retiring to rest upon Sunday night that I made up my mind to do so. The time at which I determined I would be there was one o'clock in the morning, and I also had a strong intention of making my presence perceptible.

"On the following Thursday I went to see the ladies in question, and in the course of conversation (without any allusion to the subject on my part), the elder one told me that on the previous Sunday night she had been much terrified by perceiving me standing by her bedside, and that she screamed when the apparition advanced towards her, and awoke her little sister who also saw me. I asked her if she was awake at the time, and she replied most decidedly in the affirmative; and upon my inquiring the time of the occurrence, she replied about one o'clock in the morning."

Miss Verity's account is as follows:—

"On a certain Sunday evening, about twelve months since, at our house in Hogarth Road, Kensington, I distinctly saw Mr. B. in my room about one o'clock. I was perfectly awake and was much terrified. I awoke my sister by screaming, and she saw the apparition herself. Three days after, when I saw Mr. B., I told him what had happened; but it was some time before I could recover from the shock I had received, and the remembrance is too vivid to be ever erased from my memory.

"L. S. VERITY."

Miss E. C. Verity writes:—

"I remember the occurrence of the event described by my sister in the annexed paragraph, and her description is quite correct. I saw the apparition at the same time and under the same circumstances."

Miss A. S. Verity writes:—

"I remember quite clearly the evening my eldest sister awoke me by calling to me from an adjoining room, and upon my going to her bedside, where she slept with my youngest sister, they both told me they had seen S. H. B. standing in the room. The time was about one o'clock. S. H. B. was in evening dress, they told me."

The following case, while of the same general character, presents this remarkable difference: that the agent's mind was not at all directed to the real percipient, but only to the *place* where the percipient happened to be. It is from the notebook of Mr. S. H. B. who was also the agent.

"On Friday, December 1st, 1882, at 9:30 P. M., I went into a room alone and sat by the fireside, and endeavored so strongly to fix my mind upon the interior of a house at Kew (viz., Clarence Road), in which resided Miss V. and her two sisters, that I seemed to be actually in the house.

" During this experiment I must have fallen into a mesmeric sleep, for, although I was conscious, I could not move my limbs. I did not seem to have lost the power of moving them, but I could not make the effort to do so. . . . At 10 P. M. I regained my normal state by an effort of the will and wrote down on a sheet of note-paper the foregoing statements.

"When I went to bed on this same night, I determined that I would be in the front bedroom of the above-mentioned house at 12 P.M., and remain there until I had made my presence perceptible to the inmates of that room. On the next day, Saturday, I went to Kew to spend the evening, and met there a married sister of Miss V. (viz., Mrs. L.). This lady I had only met once before and that was at a ball, two years previous to the above date. We were both in fancy dress at the time, and as we did not exchange more than half a dozen words, this lady would naturally have lost any vivid recollection of my appearance even if she had noticed it.

"In the course of conversation (although I did not for a moment think of asking her any questions on such a subject), she told me that on the previous night she had seen me distinctly on two occasions. She had spent the night at Clarence Road, and had slept in the front bedroom. At about half-past nine, she had seen me in the passage going from one room to another, and at 12 P.M., when she was wide-awake, she had seen me enter the bedroom and walk round to where she was lying and take her hair (which is very long), into my hand. She told me that the apparition took hold of her hand and gazed intently into it, whereupon she spoke, saying, 'You need not look at the lines for I have never had any trouble.'

"She then awoke her sister, Miss V., who was sleeping with her, and told her about it. After hearing this account I took the statement which I had written down the previous evening from my pocket and showed it to some of the persons present, who were much astonished, although incredulous.

"I asked Mrs. L. if she was not dreaming at the time of the latter experience, but she stoutly denied, and stated that she had forgotten what I was like, but seeing me so distinctly she recognized me at once. At my request she wrote a brief account of her impressions and signed it."

The following is the lady's statement:—

"On Friday, December 1st, 1882, I was on a visit to my sister, at 21 Clarence Road, Kew, and about 9:30 P. M. I was going from my bedroom to get some water from the bath-room, when I distinctly saw Mr. S. B. whom I had only seen once before, two years ago, walk before me past the bath-room, toward the bedroom at the end of the landing.

"About 11 o'clock we retired for the night; about 12 o'clock I was still awake, and the door opened and Mr. S. B. came into the room and walked around to the bedside, and there stood with one foot on the ground, and the other knee resting on a chair. He then took my hair into his hand, after which he took my hand in his and looked very intently into the palm. 'Ah,' I said (speaking to him), 'you need not look at the lines for I never had any trouble.' I then awoke my sister; I was not nervous, but excited, and began to fear some serious illness would befall her, she being delicate at the time, but she is progressing more favorably now.

"H. L."

(Full name signed.)

Miss Verity also corroborates this statement.

The following is still another case of one mind acting upon another mind at a distance and at least in a most unusual way. Call it mind-projection, making one's self visible at a distance, sending out the subliminal self—call it what we may—it is a glimpse of a phenomenon, rare in its occurrence, but which nevertheless has been observed a sufficient number of times to claim serious attention, and calm and candid consideration. The case is from *Phantasms of the Living*, and is furnished by "Mrs. Russell of Belgaum,

India, wife of Mr. H. R. Russell, Educational Inspector in the Bombay Presidency." It differs from those already cited in the fact that it is unconnected with either sleep or hypnotism, but both agent and percipient were awake and in a perfectly normal condition.

Mrs. Russell writes:—

"June 8th, 1886.

"As desired I write down the following facts as well as I can recall them. I was living in Scotland, my mother and sisters in Germany. I lived with a very dear friend of mine, and went to Germany every year to see my people. It had so happened that I could not go home as usual for two years, when on a sudden I made up my mind to go and see my family. They knew nothing of my intention; I had never gone in early spring before; and I had no time to let them know by letter that I was going to set off. I did not like to send a telegram for fear of frightening my mother. The thought came to me to will with all my might to appear to one of my sisters, never mind which of them, in order to give them warning of my coming. I only thought most intensely for a few minutes of them, wishing with all my might to be seen by one of them—half present myself, in vision, at home. I did not take more than ten minutes, I think. I started by the Leith steamer on Saturday night, end of April, 1859. I wished to appear at home about 6 o'clock P. M. that same Saturday.

"I arrived at home at 6 o'clock on Tuesday morning following. I entered the house without any one seeing me, the hall being cleaned and the front door open. I walked into the room. One of my sisters stood with her back to the door; she turned round when she heard the door opening, and on seeing me, stared at me, turning deadly pale, and letting what she had in her hand fall. I had been silent. Then I spoke and said, 'It is I. Why do you look so frightened?' When she answered, 'I thought I saw you again as Stinchen (another sister) saw you on Saturday.'

"When I inquired, she told me that on Saturday evening about 6 o'clock, my sister saw me quite clearly, entering the room in which she was, by one door, passing through it, opening the door of another room in which my mother was, and shutting the door behind me. She rushed after what she thought was I, calling out my name, and was quite stupefied when she did not find me with my mother. My mother could not understand my sister's excitement. They looked everywhere for me, but of course did not find me. My mother was very miserable; she thought I might be dying.

"My sister who had seen me (i. e. my apparition) was out that morning when I arrived. I sat down on the stairs to watch, when she came in, the effect of my real appearance on her. When she looked up and saw me, sitting motionless, she called out my name and nearly fainted.

"My sister had never seen anything unearthly either before that or afterwards; and I have never made any such experiments since—nor will I, as the sister that saw me first when I really came home, had a very severe illness afterwards, caused by the shock to her nerves.

J. M. RUSSELL."

Mrs. Russell's sister, in answer to her inquiry whether she remembered the incident, replied: "Of course I remember the matter as well as though it had happened to-day. Pray don't come appearing to me again!"

We started out with this proposition. Perceptions—those of the class denominated hallucinations—may have their origin telepathically. In proof and illustration of that proposition we have so far presented a single class of cases, namely,

Those where the hallucination was produced with will and purpose on the part of the agent. The cases present the following conditions:—

(1) The agent being in a normal condition—the percipient hypnotized, the hypnotic condition having been produced at a distance of a hundred yards—and from a point from which the percipient could not be seen.

(2) The agent in the hypnotic condition; a definite hallucination strongly desired and decided upon beforehand was produced, the percipient being in a normal state.

(3) The agent was in normal sleep. Hallucination decided upon before going to sleep was produced—the percipient awake and in normal condition.

(4) Both agent and percipient awake and normal—hallucination produced at a distance of four hundred miles. In one case the phantasm is seen by two percipients, and in another case the *place* only where the phantasm should appear was strongly in the agent's mind; and while the sisters who *usually* occupied that room might naturally be expected to be the percipients, as a matter of fact another person, a married sister who happened to be visiting them—a comparative stranger to the agent—was occupying the room and became the percipient.

In each of these cases a definite purpose was formed by the agent to produce a certain hallucination or present a certain picture—generally a representation or phantasm of himself to the percipient. A picture or phantasm is seen by the intended percipient, and, on comparison, in each case it is found that it is *the same phantasm* that the agent had *endeavored* to project and make visible, and that it was perceived in the same place and at the same time that the agent had intended that it should be seen.

Can these statements be received as true and reliable? In reply we say, the evidence having been carefully examined is of such a character as to entitle it to belief, and the errors of observation and reporting are trifling, and not such as would injure the credibility of statements made regarding any event which was a matter of ordinary observation; moreover, these cases now have become so numerous and have been so carefully observed that they should be judged by the ordinary rules of evidence; and by that rule they should be received.

Having been received, how can they be explained?

It may be answered:—

(1) That these apparent sequences presenting

the relation of cause and effect are merely chance coincidences. But on carefully applying the doctrine of chances, it is found that the probability that these coincidences of time and place, and the identity of the pictures presented and perceived, occurred by chance, would be only one in a number so large as to make it difficult to represent it in figures, and quite impossible for any mind to comprehend. And that such a coincidence should occur repeatedly in one person's experience is absolutely incredible.

(2) The circumstances of distance and situation render it certain that the phantasms could not have been communicated or presented to the percipient through any of the usual channels of communication—by means of the physical organs of sense — even granting that they could be so transferred under favorable conditions.

If, then, these cases must be received as authentic and true, and if they cannot be disposed of as chance coincidences, nor explained by any ordinary method or law of production or transmission, then there must be *some other* method of mental interaction, and mental intercommunication *not usually recognized*, by means of which these pictures or phantasms are produced or transferred, and this unusual method of mental interaction and intercommunication we designate *telepathy*. What the exact method is by which this unusual interaction is accomplished is not fully demonstrated, any more than are the methods of the various interacting forces between the sun and the planets or amongst the planets themselves. The hypothesis of a universal or inter-stellar ether has never been demonstrated; it is only a hypothesis framed because it is necessary in order to explain and support another undemonstrated theory, namely, the vibratory or wave theory of light. We do not know what the substance or force which we call *attraction* really is. Light has one method of movement and action, sound another, heat another, and electricity another, but most of the propositions concerning these methods of action are only theories or hypotheses having a greater or less degree of probability as the case may be. They were invented to account for certain actual and undeniable phenomena, and they are respected by all men of science or other persons having sufficient knowledge of these different subjects to entitle them to an opinion. The same thing is true of telepathy; its facts must be known and its theories well considered by those who assume to sit in judgment upon them; and when known they are respected. The Copernican theory of the planetary movements was formulated three hundred and fifty years ago; it was one hundred and fifty years later when Newton proposed the first rational theory regarding a force which might explain these motions. For this he was ridiculed and even ostracized by the self-constituted judges of his day. Telepathy has been the subject of careful study and experiment comparatively only a few years, and it can hardly, at this early date, expect better treatment at the hands of its critics. Its facts, however, remain, and its explanatory theories are being duly considered.

What, then, are the theories or hypotheses which may aid us in forming an idea of the manner in which a thought, a conception, or a mental picture may pass between two persons so situated that no communication could pass between them through the ordinary channels of communication —sight, hearing, or touch? Let us suppose two persons A and B to be so situated. A is the agent or person having unusual ability to impress his own thought, or any conception or mental picture which he may form in his own mind, upon some other mind; and B is the percipient or a person having unusual ability to receive or perceive such thoughts or mental pictures. Suppose these two people to be in the country and engaged in farming. Upon a certain morning A takes his axe and goes to the woods, half a mile distant, and is engaged in cutting brush and trees for the purpose of clearing the land, and B goes into the garden to care for the growing vegetables. After an hour spent in these respective occupations, B becomes disquieted, even alarmed, oppressed with the feeling that some misfortune has happened and that A is needing his assistance. He is unable to continue his work and at once starts for the woods to seek for A. He finds that A has received a glancing blow from his axe which has deeply wounded his foot, disabled him, and put his life in immediate danger from hemorrhage. Here the thought of A in his extreme peril goes out intensely to B, desiring his presence; and B, by some unusual perceptive power, takes cognizance of this intense thought and wish. This is telepathy. Again, suppose B hears a voice which he recognizes as A's calling his name and with a peculiar effect which B recognizes as distress or entreaty. Or, again, that B sees a picture or representation of A lying wounded and bleeding, still it is a telepathic impulse from A and taken cognizance of by B which constitutes the communication between them, whatever the exact nature or method of the communication may be.

The theories or hypotheses which have been put forward regarding the method by which this telepathic influence or impact is conveyed may be noted as follows:—

(1) That of a vibratory medium, always present and analogous to the atmosphere for propagating sound or the universal ether for propagating light.

(2) An effluence of some sort emanating from the persons concerned and acting as a medium for the time being.

(3) A sixth sense.

(4) A duplex personality or subliminal self.

First, then, as regards the vibratory hypothesis; it would demand a variety of media to convey separately something corresponding to the sense of sight, the sense of hearing, and to each of the other senses—touch, taste, and smell—as all these sensations have been telepathically transmitted, or else there must exist one single medium capable of transmitting these many widely different methods of sensation separately,—either of which suppositions are, to say the least, bewildering.

Such a medium must also possess a power of penetrating or acting through intervening obstacles, such as no medium with which we are acquainted possesses; and, lastly, in addition to numerous apparently insurmountable difficulties and insufficiencies, there is no proof whatever that any such vibratory medium exists.

Second. Regarding a vital effluence or some physical emanation or aura belonging to each individual, and by means of which communication is possible between persons separated by too great a distance to permit communication through the ordinary channels; it is at least conceivable that such an aura or personal atmosphere exists, and by some it is claimed to be demonstrated; but admitting its existence, that it would be capable of fulfilling the numerous functions demanded of it in the premises is doubtful.

Third. That the telepathic intercommunication is accomplished by means of a sixth sense—a sort of compend of all the other senses, with added powers as regards distance and intervening obstacles—is a hypothesis which has been urged by some, and is at least intelligible; but, while it presents an intelligible explanation of such facts as clairvoyance and the hearing of voices, there is a large class of facts, as we shall see, which utterly refuse to fall into line or be explained by this hypothesis.

Fourth. The hypothesis of different strata of personality—or of a second or subliminal self—is the one which best fulfils the necessary conditions and also harmonizes the greatest number of facts when arranged with reference to this idea. There is also real, substantial evidence that such a second personality actually exists, some of the facts bearing upon this subject having been presented in former chapters.

Those of my readers who have carefully followed the cases of unusual mental action there presented —cases of thought-transference, of clairvoyance, of remarkable mind-action in the hypnotic trance and in natural somnambulism—in well marked examples of double consciousness as shown in the cases of Félida X., of Alma Z., of Ansel Bourne, and the hypnotic subject, Madame B., in her various personalities of Léonie, Léontine, and Léonore, in automatic action as displayed in Planchette-writing, in trance-speaking and in crystal-gazing, cannot have failed to observe, throughout the whole series, mind acting rationally and intelligently, quite independently of the ordinary consciousness, and even at times independently of the whole physical organization. We have considered the evidence which points to the fact, or at least to the theory of a subliminal self, or another personality, in some manner bound up in that complicated physical and mental mechanism which constitutes what we term an individual. We have seen that there are weighty proofs that such a secondary or subliminal, or, if you choose so to designate it, *supranormal* self, actually exists, and that it exhibits functions and powers far exceeding the functions and powers of the ordinary self. We have seen it expressing its own personal opinions, its own likes and dislikes, quite different and opposite to the opinions, likes, and dislikes of the ordinary self; having its own separate series of remembered actions or chain of memories, its own antecedent history, and its separate present interests; and especially performing actions altogether beyond the powers of the ordinary self. We have seen it going out to great distances, seeing and describing scenes and events there taking place—for example, Swedenborg at Gottenburg witnessing the conflagration at Stockholm; Dr. Gerault's clairvoyant maid-servant, Marie, in France, seeing the sad death of her neighbor's son, Limoges, the ropemaker, while serving in the Crimea; and also the serious illness of Dr. Gerault's military friend in Algiers. Fitzgerald, at Brunswick, Me., seeing and describing the Fall River fire three hundred miles away, and Mrs. Porter, at Bridgeport, Conn., describing the burning of the steamer *Henry Clay* while it was occurring on the Hudson River near the village of Yonkers. We have seen this same subliminal self in the case of Mr. Stead, going out and acquiring desired knowledge relating to the location, occupation, and needs of persons from whom he desired such information, and bringing it back and reporting it by means of automatic writing. Again, we have seen this subliminal self in the case of Mrs. Newnham, perceiving the silently written and sometimes even the unwritten questions of her husband, and automatically writing the answers by means of Planchette; and we have seen it producing hallucinations of hearing as in the case of Léonore causing Léontine to hear a voice reproving her for her flippancy.

A remarkable series of facts are here pointed out, facts some of which are akin to those which have for ages been lying about in the lumber rooms of history or in out-of-the-way corners of men's memories, neglected and discredited, because unexplained, unaccounted for, forming no part of any recognized system of mental action, and some only recently observed and even now looked at askance for the same reason. They have remained a mass of undigested and unarranged facts, without system, without any ascertained relation to each other, pointing to no definite principle, defined by no definite law. It is only within the past decade that these facts have been studied with reference to the action of a subliminal self.

But this new and startling idea being once admitted and brought to the front, it is found that not only in the whole series of observed automatic actions in the somnambulism of the hypnotic state, and that of ordinary sleep, are the organs of the unconscious body made use of by this subconscious or subliminal self, but also in dreams, in reverie, in moments of abstraction, of strong emotion or mental excitement, and even in the case of some peculiarly susceptible persons in the ordinary waking condition, this subliminal self can greatly influence and sometimes take entire control of the action of the body.

It will be seen then, how wide and important is the range of phenomena in which the subliminal self appears as an active agent, impressing its own special knowledge, however acquired, its ideas, pictures, and images upon the primary self, and causing them to be perceived, remembered, and

KEY TO THE PHENOMENA. 261

expressed by it; and with this unusual power in view, evidently it is in this direction also that we must look for the key to that still more remarkable series of phenomena which are known as phantasms or apparitions.

CHAPTER XI.

PHANTASMS CONTINUED.

So far a single class of cases has been brought forward in proof and illustration of our proposition, that *sensation may be produced telepathically*, namely, the voluntary class; as for instance, when it has been resolved beforehand and strongly desired and willed that a representation or apparition of one's self should be seen and recognized by another person at a specified time and place, and it has been so recognized. This class contains fewer recorded cases, but, on the other hand, they are specially valuable, because the element of error arising from chance coincidence is almost entirely excluded. In addition to these voluntary or prearranged cases there is, however, another and much larger class of cases which occur spontaneously, unthought of, and unexpected by the percipient as well as by the agent.

Passing over cases of an indefinite or undefined

sense of danger or peril—or of a " presence "—we will proceed to notice some well authenticated cases of spontaneous impressions of a definite character made upon the senses, and especially upon the sense of sight. This definite impression may be made upon the senses of the percipient in dreams—especially those of a veridical character, where there is a definite reality corresponding in time and circumstances.

It may also be made when the percipient is in a condition of reverie, between sleeping and waking, and even when wide awake and in a perfectly normal condition.

This definite impression of seeing or hearing may be made upon a single percipient, or it may be perceived by several persons at once.

The following may serve as examples of *veridical dreams*. They were carefully examined by the editors of *Phantasms of the Living*, and especially by Mr. Gurney. Only initials in the first case were given for publication.

" In the year 1857, I had a brother in the very centre of the Indian Mutiny. I had been ill in the spring and taken from my lessons in the school-room, consequently, I heard more of what was going on from the newspapers than a girl of thirteen ordinarily would in those days.

We were in the habit of hearing regularly from my brother, but in June and July of that year no letters came, and what arrived in August proved to have been written quite early in the spring, and were full of disturbances around his station.

"He was in the service of the East India Company—an officer in the 8th Native Infantry. I was always devoted to him, and I grieved and fretted far more than any of my elders knew at his danger. I cannot say that I dreamt constantly of him, but when I did the impressions were very vivid and abiding.

"On one occasion his personal appearance was being discussed and I remarked, 'He is not like that now, he has no beard nor whiskers;' and when asked why I said such a thing, I replied, 'I know it, for I have seen him in my dreams;' and this brought a severe reprimand from my governess, who never allowed 'such nonsense' to be talked of.

"On the morning of the 25th of September, quite early, I awoke from a dream, to find my sister holding me and much alarmed. I had screamed and struggled, crying out, 'Is he really dead?' When I fully awoke, I felt a burning sensation in my head. I could not speak for a moment or two; I knew my sister was there, but I neither saw nor felt her.

"In about a minute, during which she said my eyes were staring beyond her, I ceased struggling cried out, 'Harry's dead, they have shot him,' and fainted. When I recovered I found my sister had been sent away, and an aunt who had always looked after me, was sitting by my bed.

"In order to soothe my excitement, she allowed me to tell my dream, trying all the time to persuade me to regard it as a natural consequence of my anxiety.

"When, in my narration, I said he was riding with another officer and mounted soldiers behind them, she exclaimed 'My dear, that shows you it is only a dream, for your brother is in an *infantry*, not a cavalry, regiment.'

"Nothing, however, shook my feeling that I had seen a reality; and she was so much struck by my persistence that she privately made notes of the dates and of the incidents, even to the minutest details of my dream, and then for a few days the matter dropped, but I felt the truth was coming nearer and nearer to all. In a short time the news came in the papers :—'Shot down on the morning of the 25th, when on his way to Lucknow.' A few days later came one of his missing letters, telling how his own regiment had mutinied, and that he had been transferred to a command in the 12th Irregular Cavalry, bound to join Havelock's force in the relief of Lucknow.

"Some eight years after, the officer who was riding by him when he fell, Captain or Major Grant, visited us and when, in compliance with my aunt's request, he detailed the incidents of that sad hour, his narration tallied (even to the description of buildings on their left) with the notes she had taken the morning of my dream. I should also add that we heard my brother had made the alteration in his beard and whiskers, just about the time that I had spoken of him as wearing them differently."

"L. A. W."

The next case which I will present is from Dr. A. K. Young, F. R. C. S. I., of the Terrace, Monaghan, Ireland.

One Monday night, in December, 1836, Dr. Young had the following dream, or, as he would prefer to call it, revelation. He found himself suddenly at the gate of Major N. M.'s avenue, many miles from his home. Close to him was a group of persons, one of them a woman with a basket on her arm, the rest men, four of whom were tenants of his own, while the others were unknown to him. Some of the strangers seemed to be murderously assaulting H. W., one of his tenants, and he interfered. He goes on to say:

"I struck violently at the man on my left and then with greater violence at the man's face to my right. Finding to my surprise that I did not knock him down either, I struck again and again with all the violence of a man frenzied at the sight of my poor friend's murder. To my great amazement I saw that my arms, although visible to my eye, were without substance; and the bodies of the men I struck at and my own came close together after each blow through the shadowy arms I struck with. My blows were delivered with more extreme violence than I ever before exerted; but I became painfully convinced of my incompetency. I have no consciousness of what happened after this feeling of unsubstantiality came upon me."

Next morning, Dr. Young experienced the stiffness and soreness of violent bodily exercise and was informed by his wife that in the course of the night he had much alarmed her by striking out again and again with his arms in a terrific manner, "as if fighting for his life." He in turn informed her of his dream and begged her to remember the names of the actors in it who were known to him.

On the morning of the following day, Wednesday, he received a letter from his agent, who resided in the town close to the scene of his dream, informing him that his tenant, H. W., had been found on Tuesday morning at Major N. M.'s gate speechless and apparently dying from a fracture of the skull, and that there was no trace of the murderers. That night Dr. Young started for the town and arrived there on Thursday morning. On his way to a meeting of the magistrates he met the senior magistrate of that part of the country and requested him to give orders for the arrest of the three men whom, besides H. W., he had recognized in his dream, and to have them examined separately. This was done. The three men gave identical accounts of the occurrence, and all named the woman who was with them. She was then arrested and gave precisely similar testimony.

They said that between eleven and twelve on Monday night they had been walking homeward, all together along the road, when they were overtaken by three strangers, two of whom savagely assaulted H. W., while the other prevented his friends from interfering. The man H. W. did not die, and no clue was ever found to the assassins.

The Bishop of Clogher writes confirmatory of Dr. Young's account.

"Borderland cases" are those in which the percipient, though seeming to himself to be awake, may be in bed, has perhaps been asleep, and is in that condition between sleeping and waking known as reverie and which we have seen is favorable for the action of the subliminal self, either as agent or percipient.

Passing, then, from dreams to "Borderland cases," the first example under this head which I will present is from Mrs. Richardson, of Combe Down, Bath, England.

She writes:—

"August 26th, 1882.

"On September 9th, 1848, at the Siege of Mooltan, my husband, Major-General Richardson, C. B., then adjutant of his regiment, was most severely wounded, and supposing himself dying, asked one of the officers with him to take the ring off his finger and send it to his wife, who at that time was fully one hundred and fifty miles distant, at Ferozepore. On the night of September 9th, 1848, I was lying in my bed between sleeping and waking, when I distinctly saw my husband being carried off the field seriously wounded, and heard his voice saying, 'Take this ring off my finger and send it to my wife.'

"All the next day I could not get the sight nor the voice out of my mind. In due time I heard of Gen. Richardson having been severely wounded in the assault on Mooltan. He survived, however, and is still living. It was not for some time after the siege that I heard from Colonel L., the officer who helped to carry Gen. Richardson off the field, that the request as to the ring was actually made to him, just as I had heard it at Ferozepore at that very time.

"M. A. RICHARDSON."

The following questions were addressed to Gen. Richardson.

1. "Does Gen. Richardson remember saying, when he was wounded at Mooltan, 'Take this ring off my finger and send it to my wife,' or words to that effect?"

Ans. "Most distinctly; I made the request to my commanding officer, Major E. S. Lloyd, who was supporting me while my man was gone for assistance."

2. "Can you remember the *time* of the incident?"

Ans. "So far as my memory serves me, I was wounded about nine P. M., on Sunday, the 9th September, 1848."

3. "Had Gen. Richardson, before he left home, promised or said anything to Mrs. R. as to sending his ring to her in case he should be wounded?"

Ans. "To the best of my recollection, never. Nor had I any kind of presentiment on the subject. I naturally felt that with such a fire as we were exposed to, I might get hurt."

The next case is from Miss Hosmer, the celebrated sculptor. It was written out by Miss Balfour, from the account given by Lydia Maria Child, and corrected by Miss Hosmer, July 15th, 1885.

"An Italian girl named Rosa was in my employ for some time, but was finally obliged to return home to her sister on account of confirmed ill-health. When I took my customary exercise on horseback, I frequently called to see her. On one of these occasions I called about six o'clock P. M., and found her brighter than I had seen her for some time past. I had long relinquished hopes of her recovery, but there was nothing in her appearance that gave me the impression of immediate danger. I left her with the expectation of calling to see her again many times. She expressed a wish to have a bottle of a certain kind of wine, which I promised to bring her myself next morning.

"During the remainder of the evening I do not recollect that Rosa was in my thoughts after I parted with her. I retired to rest in good health and in a quiet frame of mind. But I woke from a sound sleep with an oppressive feeling that some one was in the room.

"I reflected that no one could get in except my maid, who had the key to one of the two doors of my room—both of which doors were locked. I was able dimly to distinguish the furniture in the room. My bed was in the middle of the room with a screen around the foot of it. Thinking some one might be behind the screen I said, 'Who's there?' but got no answer. Just then the clock in the adjacent room struck five; and at that moment I saw the figure of Rosa standing by my bedside; and in some way, though I could not venture to say it was through the medium of speech, the impression was conveyed to me from her of these words: 'Adesso son felice, son contenta.' And with that the figure vanished.

"At the breakfast table I said to the friend who shared the apartment with me, 'Rosa is dead.' 'What do you mean by that?' she inquired; 'you told me she seemed better yesterday.' I related the occurrence of the morning and told her I had a strong impression Rosa was dead. She laughed and said I had dreamed it all. I assured her I was thoroughly awake. She continued to jest on the subject and slightly annoyed me by her persistence in believing it a dream when I was perfectly sure of having been wide awake. To settle the question I summoned a messenger, and sent him to inquire how Rosa did. He returned with the answer that she died that morning at five o'clock.

"H. G. HOSMER."

I will also introduce here as a "Borderland case" an extract from *The Life and Times of Lord Brougham, written by himself* (1871), the extract being an entry in his journal during a journey in Sweden in December, 1799. It is as follows:—

"We set out for Gothenburg [apparently on December 18th], determined to make for Norway. About one in the morning, arriving at a decent inn, we decided to stop over night. Tired with the cold of yesterday, I was glad to take advantage of a hot bath before I turned in, and here a most remarkable thing happened to me—so remarkable that I must tell the story from the beginning.

"After I left the High School, I went with G., my most intimate friend, to attend the classes at the University. There was no divinity class, but we frequently in our walks discussed and speculated upon many grave subjects—among others, on the immortality of the soul, and a future state. This question, and the possibility, I will not say of ghosts walking, but of the dead appearing to the living, were subjects of much speculation; and we actually committed the folly of drawing up an agreement written with our blood, to the effect that which ever of us died first should appear to the other, and thus solve any doubts we had entertained of the 'life after death.' After we had finished our classes at college, G. went to India, having got an appointment there in the Civil Service.

"He seldom wrote to me, and after the lapse of a few years I had almost forgotten him; moreover, his family having little connection with Edinburgh, I seldom saw or heard anything of them, or of him through them, so that all his school-boy intimacy had died out, and I had nearly forgotten his existence. I had taken, as I have said, a warm bath, and while lying in it and enjoying the comfort of the heat after the late freezing I had undergone, I turned my head round, looking towards the chair on which I had deposited my clothes, as I was about to get out of the bath. On the chair sat G, looking calmly at me.

"How I got out of the bath I know not, but on recovering my senses I found myself sprawling on the floor. The apparition, or whatever it was that had taken the likeness of G., had disappeared.

"This vision produced such a shock that I had no inclination to talk about it even to Stewart; but the impression it made upon me was too vivid to be easily forgotten; and so strongly was I affected by it that I have here written down the whole history, with the date, 19th December, and all the particulars, as they are now fresh before me.

"No doubt I had fallen asleep; and that the appearance presented so distinctly to my eyes was a dream, I cannot for a moment doubt; yet for years I had had no communication with G., nor had there been anything to recall him to my recollection; nothing had taken place during our Swedish travels either connected with G. or with India, or with anything relating to him, or to any member of his family. I could not discharge from my mind the impression that G. must have died, and that his appearance to me was to be received as a proof of a future state; yet all the while I felt convinced that the whole was a dream; and so painfully vivid, so unfading the impression, that I could not bring myself to talk of it or make the slightest allusion to it."

In October, 1862, Lord Brougham added as a postscript :—

"I have just been copying out from my journal the account of this strange dream: *Certissima mortis imago!* And now to finish the story, begun about sixty years ago. Soon after my return to Edinburgh, there arrived a letter from India, announcing G.'s death, and stating that he had died on the 19th of December!

"Singular coincidence! Yet, when one reflects on the vast number of dreams which night after night pass through our brains, the number of coincidences between the vision and the event are perhaps fewer and less remarkable than a fair calculation of chances would warrant us to expect. Nor is it surprising, considering the variety of thoughts in sleep, and that they all bear some analogy to the affairs of life, that a dream should sometimes coincide with a contemporaneous, or even with a future, event. This is not much more wonderful than that a person whom we have had no reason to expect should appear to us at the very moment we have been thinking or speaking of him. So common is this, that it has for ages grown into the proverb, 'Speak of the devil.' I believe every such seeming miracle is, like every ghost story, capable of explanation."

I have introduced in full Lord Brougham's statement of the case and his method of reasoning upon it; let us for a moment analyze each.

I have also introduced Harriet Hosmer's experience along with that of Lord Brougham, because they are both notable persons whose evidence regarding matters of fact could not be impugned, and whose strength of character, honesty of purpose, and knowledge of affairs enables us to throw out of account any idea of imposture or self-deception in either case. These cases, then, must be received as having actually occurred as related; and being so received they render all the more credible other cases reported by persons less well known.

What was the character of the apparitions or appearances which were presented; were they, properly speaking, dreams? In Miss Hosmer's statement she stoutly affirms that she was awake, and she gives good reasons for so believing, namely, before she *saw* anything, but only *felt* that some one was in the room, she *awoke* from a sound sleep; she reasoned with herself regarding the possibility of any one getting into the room; she called out: "Who's there?" She saw the furniture, heard the clock strike, and counted five; and in another account which I also have, she heard the familiar noises about the house of servants at their usual work, and she resolved to get up. All this before she saw anything unusual; then turning her head she saw Rosa. Clearly this was not a dream but a vision occurring possibly in a condition of reverie.

Taking up Lord Brougham's case: in simply recording the facts in his diary he speaks of his experience as a *vision* and the idea that it was a *dream* was evidently an after-thought. He was *enjoying* the heat; he was *about to get out of the bath;* he *turned* his head. He describes the sensations and actions of a man who is awake, or certainly not in a condition to have dreams disconnected with his actual surroundings. After all this, looking toward the chair upon which he had deposited his clothes—still a part of his surroundings, of which he was perfectly conscious—he saw G. on the chair *looking calmly at him*.

Now to have *dreamt* of G., his old school-fellow and friend, looking calmly at him, would not have been anything shocking nor even surprising; it would not have been even *uncommon* among dreams—it would have been nothing out of the ordinary course of nature. Dreams seldom shock or even surprise us—surely not unless there is something intrinsically shocking represented by them; but when we see the phantasm of a person whom we know cannot be there—that is unusual, that is not in the ordinary course of nature, as we are accustomed to observe nature, and it surprises us, shocks us, perhaps frightens us; but it does so because we are awake and can reason about it and compare its strangeness with the usual order of things.

Lord Brougham was awake, he did so reason, and was accordingly shocked.

So vivid was the apparition that he tumbled out of the bath and fainted. It is only some time after this, when writing up his diary, that he has no doubt that he had fallen asleep. Preconceived theories about apparitions now come up in his mind and get him into trouble; he must *explain* his vision.

Now for the explanation. Lord Brougham finds, on returning to Scotland, that his former friend is dead, and that the time of his death corresponded with the time at which he had seen his apparition in Sweden, December 19th.

"Singular coincidence!" That is Lord Brougham's explanation; and that is the usual explanation; but it is ill-considered—it is weak—it does not cover the ground.

Lord Brougham had but two theories from which to choose: namely, Chance and Supernaturalism; and of the two horns of the dilemma he chose the easier one.

Let us, however, place ourselves, for the moment, on his ground, namely, that (1) It was a dream; and (2) dreams are so numerous that it is not surprising that some of them coincide with contemporaneous events.

Evidently the more numerous the coincidences, or the dreams which correspond to contemporaneous events, the weaker becomes the theory of *chance* coincidences. Supposing, then, Lord Brougham's case to have been unique, that not another similar case was known to have occurred, then we should have no particular hesitation in assigning it to the category of chance coincidences; but even then it would be out of the order of *usual* coincidences both in interest and the number of separate points involved; it would excite special interest, but the reference of it to chance would not be considered unreasonable: if, however, three or four such cases had been reported and discussed in a generation, thoughtful people would begin to inquire if there might not be some relation of sequence, or possibly of cause and effect ; but when hundreds of cases have been reported, because they have been systematically sought for—veridical dreams connected with the moment of the death of the agent, with fainting, with trance, with moments of supreme excitement, or of extreme danger, so many different conditions in which by careful observation it is found that such hallucinations and symbols relating to actual contemporaneous occurrences originate and are telepathically transmitted—the matter is then quite removed from the category of chance coincidences, and any attempt to force these cases there to-day denotes either ignorance of established facts or inability to appreciate logical reasoning or even mathematical demonstration. This is all upon the supposition that the case in question was a dream. On the other hand, now place the case where it really belongs as a *waking* or Borderland *vision*—an event in a class a hundred-fold less numerous than dreams— and in which class corresponding events are at least tenfold *more numerous*, and we see how conspicuously weak is the coincidence theory.

Neither need the other horn of the dilemma,

namely, Supernaturalism, any longer be taken. A newly recognized method of mental interaction is gradually coming into view; a new principle and law in psychology is being established; and under this law the erratic and discredited facts of history as well as the facts of present observation and experiment are falling into line and becoming intelligible.

The new principle or law, as we have seen, is this: Perceptions, of the class which have usually been known as hallucinations, may be originated and transferred *telepathically;* in other words, there is a subliminal self, which, under various conditions on the part of either agent or percipient, or both, may come to the surface and act, impressing the sensitive percipient through the senses, by dreams, visions, and apparitions, as well as through hallucinations of hearing and touch.

Returning to our well considered cases illustrating some of these various conditions: having presented examples of veridical or truth-telling dreams, and of waking or borderland visions also corresponding to actual events taking place at the same time, I will next present cases where the percipient was *undoubtedly awake* and in a normal condition. The following case is reported on the authority of Surgeon Harris of the Royal Artillery, who, with his two daughters, was a witness of the occurrence:

"A party of children, sons and daughters of the officers of artillery stationed at Woolwich, were playing in the garden. Suddenly a little girl screamed, and stood staring with an aspect of terror at a willow tree standing in the grounds. Her companions gathered round, asking what ailed her. 'Oh!' said she, 'there—there. Don't you see? There's papa lying on the ground, and the blood running from a big wound.' All assured her that they could see nothing of the kind. But she persisted, describing the wound and the position of the body, still expressing surprise that they did not see what she so plainly saw. Two of her companions were daughters of one of the surgeons of the regiment, whose house adjoined the garden. They called their father, who at once came to the spot. He found the child in a state of extreme terror and agony, took her into his house, assured her it was only a fancy, and having given her restoratives sent her home. The incident was treated by all as what the doctor had called it, a fancy, and no more was thought of it. News from India, where the child's father was stationed, was in those days slow in coming, but the arrival of the mail in due course brought the information that the father of the child had been killed by a shot, and died under a tree. Making allowances for difference in time, it was found to have been about the moment when the daughter had the vision at Woolwich."

The next case is from Mr. Francis Dart Fenton, formerly in the native department of the Government, Auckland, New Zealand. In 1852, when the incident occurred, Mr. Fenton was engaged in forming a settlement on the banks of the Waikato.

He writes:—

"March 25th, 1860.

"Two sawyers, Frank Philps and Jack Mulholland, were engaged cutting timber for the Rev. R. Maunsell, at the mouth of the Awaroa Creek, a very lonely place, a vast swamp, no people within miles of them. As usual, they had a Maori with them to assist in felling trees. He came from Tihorewam, a village on the other side of the river, about six miles off. As Frank and the native were cross-cutting a tree, the native stopped suddenly and said, 'What are you come for?' looking in the direction of Frank. Frank replied, 'What do you mean?' He said, 'I am not speaking to you; I am speaking to my brother.' Frank said, 'Where is he?' The native replied,

'Behind you. What do you want?' (to the other Maori). Frank looked round and saw nobody; the native no longer saw any one, but laid down the saw and said, 'I shall go across the river; my brother is dead.' Frank laughed at him, and reminded him that he had left him quite well on Sunday (five days before), and there had been no communication since. The Maori spoke no more, but got into his canoe and pulled across. When he arrived at the landing-place, he met people coming to fetch him. His brother had just died. I knew him well."

In answer to inquiries as to his authority for this narrative, Mr. Fenton writes the editors of *Phantasms of the Living* :—

"December 18th, 1883.

"I knew all the parties well, and it is quite true. Incidents of this sort are not infrequent among the Maoris.

"F. D. FENTON,

"Late Chief Judge, Native Law Court of New Zealand."

The following case was first published in the *Spiritual Magazine* in 1861, by Robert H. Collyer, M. D., F. C. S.

Although published in a spiritual publication, Dr. Collyer states that he himself is not a believer in spiritualism, but, on the contrary, is a materialist and has been for forty years.

He writes from Beta House, 8 Alpha Road, St. John's Wood, N. W. :—

"April 15th, 1861.

"On January 3d, 1856, my brother Joseph being in command of the steamer *Alice*, on the Mississippi, just above New Orleans, she came in collision with another steamer. The concussion caused the flagstaff or pole to fall with great violence, which coming in contact with my brother's head, actually divided the skull, causing of necessity instant death. In October, 1857, I visited the United States. When at my father's residence, Camden, New Jersey, the melancholy death of my brother became the subject of conversation, and my mother narrated to me that at the very time of the accident the apparition of my brother Joseph was presented to her. This fact was corroborated by my father and four sisters. Camden, N. J., is distant from the scene of the accident, in a direct line, over one thousand miles. My mother mentioned the fact of the apparition on the morning of the 4th of January to my father and sisters; nor was it until the 16th, or thirteen days after, that a letter was received confirming in every particular the extraordinary visitation. It will be important to mention that my brother William and his wife lived near the locality of the dreadful accident, and are now living in Philadelphia; they have also corroborated to me the details of the impression produced upon my mother."

Dr. Collyer then quotes a letter from his mother which contains the following sentences:—

"CAMDEN, N. J., UNITED STATES,
"March 27th, 1861.

"MY BELOVED SON,—On the 3d of January, 1856, I did not feel well and retired early to bed. Some time after I felt uneasy and sat up in bed; I looked around the room, and to my utter amazement, saw Joseph standing at the door looking at me with great earnestness; his head was bandaged up, a dirty night-cap on, and a dirty white garment, something like a surplice. He was much disfigured about the eyes and face. It made me quite uncomfortable the rest of the night. The next morning Mary came into my room early. I told her I was sure I was going to have bad news from Joseph. I told all the family at the breakfast table. They replied, 'It was only a dream and nonsense;' but that did not change my opinion. It preyed on my mind, and on the 16th of January I received the news of his death; and singular to say both William and his wife, who were there, say that he was exactly attired as I saw him.

"Your ever affectionate mother,
"ANNE E. COLLYER."

In reply to questions, Dr Collyer wrote: "My father, who was a scientific man, calculated the difference of longitude between Camden and New Orleans and found that the mental impression was at the exact time of my brother's death. . . .

"In the published account I omitted to state that my brother Joseph, prior to his death, had retired for the night in his berth; his vessel was moored alongside the levee, at the time of the collision by another steamer coming down the Mississippi. Of course my brother was in his *nightgown*. He ran on deck on being called and informed that a steamer was in close proximity to his own. These circumstances were communicated to me by my brother William, who was on the spot at the time of the accident."

In addition to these accounts, Mr. Podmore says:—

"I called upon Dr. Collyer on March 25th, 1884. He told me that he received a full account of the story verbally from his father, mother, and brother in 1857. . . . He was quite certain of the precise coincidence of time."

A sister also writes corroborating all the main statements.

Other senses besides that of sight may receive the telepathic impression. In the following cases the sense of hearing was so impressed. The first account is from Commander T. W. Aylesbury, late of the Indian Navy. It is from Mr. Gurney's collection in *Phantasms of the Living*.

" The writer when thirteen years of age was capsized in a boat when landing on the Island of Bally, east of Java, and was nearly drowned. On coming to the surface after being repeatedly submerged, the boy called out for his mother. This amused the boat's crew, who spoke of it afterwards and jeered him a good deal about it. Months after, on arrival in England, the boy went to his home, and while telling his mother of his narrow escape he said, ' While I was under the water I saw you all sitting in this room; you were working on something white. I saw you all—mother, Emily, Eliza, and Ellen.' His mother at once said, ' Why, yes, and I *heard* you cry out for me, and I sent Emily to look out of the window, for I remarked that something had happened to that poor boy.' The time, owing to the difference in longitude, corresponded with the time when the voice was heard."

Commander Aylesbury adds in another letter:

"I saw their features (my mother's and sisters'), the room and the furniture, and particularly the old-fashioned Venetian blinds. My eldest sister was seated next to my mother."

The following is an extract from a letter written to Commander Aylesbury by one of his sisters and forwarded to Mr. Gurney, in 1883:—

"I distinctly remember the incident you mention in your letter (the voice calling 'Mother'); it made such an impression upon my mind I shall never forget it. We were all sitting quietly at work one evening; it was about nine o'clock. I think it must have been late in the summer, as we had left the street door open. We first heard a faint cry of 'Mother'; we all looked up and said to one another, 'Did you hear that? some one cried out "Mother."' We had scarcely finished speaking when the voice again called 'Mother' twice in quick succession, the last cry a frightened, agonizing cry. We all started up and mother said to me, 'Go to the door and see what is the matter.' I ran directly into the street and stood some few minutes, but all was silent, and not a person to be seen; it was a lovely evening, not a breath of air. Mother was sadly upset about it. I remember she paced the room and feared something had happened to you. She wrote down the date the next day, and when you came home and told us how nearly you had been drowned, and the time of day, father said it would be about the time nine o'clock would be with us. I know the date and the time corresponded."

In the next case three of the senses—sight, hearing, and touch were concerned. It is from Mr. Gurney's collection.

"From Mr. Algeron Joy, 20 Walton Place, S. W.
"Aug. 16th, 1883.

"About 1862 I was walking in a country lane near Cardiff by myself, when I was overtaken by two young colliers who suddenly attacked me. One of them gave me a violent blow on the eye which knocked me down, half-stunned. I distinctly remembered afterwards all that I had been thinking about, both immediately prior to the attack and for some time after it.

Up to the moment of the attack and for some time previously, I was absorbed in a calculation connected with Penarth Docks, then in construction, on which I was employed. My train of thought was interrupted for a moment by the sound of footsteps behind me. I looked back and saw the two young men, but thought no more of them, and immediately returned to my calculations.

"On receiving the blow, I began speculating on their object, what they were going to do next, how I could best defend myself, or escape from them; and when they ran away, and I had picked myself up I thought of trying to identify them and of denouncing them at the police station, to which I proceeded after following them until I lost sight of them.

"In short, I am positive that for about half an hour previous to the attack, and for an hour or two after it, there was no connection whatever, direct or indirect, between my thoughts and a person at that moment in London, and whom I will call 'A.'

"Two days afterwards, I received a letter from 'A,' written on the day after the assault, asking me what I had been doing and thinking about at 4 : 30 P. M., on the day previous to that on which he was writing. He continued: 'I had just passed your club and was thinking of you, when I recognized your footstep behind me. You laid your hand heavily on my shoulder. I turned, and saw you as distinctly as I ever saw you in my life. You looked distressed, and in answer to my greeting and inquiry, 'What's the matter?' You said, 'Go home, old fellow, I've been hurt. You will get a letter from me in the morning, telling you all about it.' You then vanished instantaneously.

"The assault took place as near 4:30 as possible, certainly between 4:15 and 4:45. I wrote an account of it to 'A' on the following day, so our letters crossed, he receiving mine, not the next morning as my *double* had promised, but on the succeeding one at about the same time as I received his. 'A' solemnly assured me that he knew no one in or near Cardiff, and that my account was the only one he had received of the incident. From my intimate personal knowledge of him I am certain that he is incapable of uttering an untruth. But there are reasons why I cannot give his name even in confidence.

"ALGERON JOY."

Apparitions are perhaps more frequently seen by a single percipient; there are, however, numerous well authenticated cases where they have been seen by several persons at the same time, sometimes by the whole and sometimes only by a part of the persons present.

Such cases are called *collective*. Here are two such cases reported to Mr. Gurney by physicians.

First, one from Dr. Wyld, 41 Courtfield Road, S. W.

"December, 1882.

"Miss L. and her mother were for fifteen years my most intimate friends; they were ladies of the highest intelligence and perfectly truthful, and their story was confirmed by one of the servants, the other I could not trace.

"Miss L., some years before I made her acquaintance, occupied much of her time in visiting the poor. One day as she walked homewards she felt cold and tired and longed to be at home warming herself at the kitchen fire. At or about the minute corresponding to this wish, the two servants being in the kitchen, the door-handle was seen to turn, the door opened, and in walked Miss L., and going up to the fire she held out her hands and warmed herself, and the servants saw she had a pair of *green* kid gloves on her hands. She suddenly disappeared before their eyes, and the two servants in great alarm went upstairs and told the mother what they had seen, including the green kid gloves. The mother feared something was wrong, but she attempted to quiet the servants by reminding them that Miss L. always wore black and never green gloves, and that therefore the 'ghost' could not have been that of her daughter.

"In about half an hour the veritable Miss L. entered the house, and going into the kitchen warmed herself at the fire; and she had on a pair of *green* kid gloves which she had bought on her way home, not being able to get a suitable black pair.

"G. WYLD, M. D."

The next case is from Dr. Wm. M. Buchanan, 12 Rutland Square, Edinburgh.

He writes:—

"The following circumstance took place at a villa about one and a half miles from Glasgow, and was told me by my wife. Of its truth I am as certain as if I had been a witness. The house had a lawn in front of about three or four acres in extent, with a lodge at the gateway distinctly seen from the house, which was about eighty yards' distant. Two of the family were going to visit a friend seven miles' distant, and on the previous day it had been arranged to take a lady, Miss W., with them, who was to be in waiting at a place about a mile distant. Three of the family and a lady visitor were standing at one of the dining-room windows waiting for the carriage, when they, including my wife, saw Miss W. open the gate at the lodge. The wind had disarranged the front of a pelisse which she wore, which they distinctly saw her adjust. She wore a light gray-colored beaver hat, and had a handkerchief at her mouth; it was supposed she was suffering from toothache to which she was subject. She entered the lodge to the surprise of her friends, and as she did not leave it, a servant was sent to ask her to join the family; but she was informed that Miss W. had not been there, and it was afterwards ascertained that no one except the woman's husband had been in the lodge that morning.

"The carriage arrived at the house about ten A. M., and Miss W. was found at the place agreed upon, in the dress in which she appeared at the lodge, and suffering from toothache. As she was a nervous person, nothing was said to her about her appearance at the gate. She died nine years afterwards."

Sometimes an apparition seemingly intended for one person is not perceived by that person, but is seen by some other person present who may be a stranger to the agent or person whose image is seen. The following case is in point. It is from Mrs. Clerke, of Clifton Lodge, Farquhar Road, Upper Norwood, S. E., and also belongs to Mr. Gurney's collection:—

"In the month of August, 1864, about three or four o'clock in the afternoon, I was sitting reading in the verandah of our house in Barbadoes. My black nurse was driving my little girl, about eighteen months or so old, in her perambulator in the garden. I got up after some time to go into the house, not having noticed anything at all, when this black woman said to me, 'Missis, who was that gentleman that was talking to you just now?' 'There was no one talking to me,' I said. 'Oh, yes, dere was, Missis—a very pale gentleman, very tall, and he talked to you and you was very rude, for you never answered him.' I repeated there was no one, and got rather cross with the woman, and she begged me to write down the day, for she knew she had seen some one. I did, and in a few days I heard of the death of my brother in Tobago. Now the curious part is this, that I did not see him, but she—a stranger to him—did; and she said that he seemed very anxious for me to notice him.

"May Clerke."

In answer to inquiries Mrs. Clerke says:—

"(1) The day of the death was the same, for I wrote it down. I think it was the third of August, but I know it was the same.

"(2) The description 'very tall and pale' was accurate.

"(3) I had no idea he was ill. He was only a few days ill.

"(4) The woman had never seen him. She had been with me about eighteen months and I considered her truthful. She had no object in telling me."

Her husband, Colonel Clerke, corroborates as follows:—

"I well remember that on the day on which Mr. John Brersford, my wife's brother, died in Tobago —after a short illness of which we were not aware —our black nurse declared she saw, at as nearly as possible the time of his death, a gentleman exactly answering to Mr. Brersford's description, leaning over the back of Mrs. Clerke's easy-chair in the open verandah. The figure was not seen by any one else.

"SHADWELL H. CLERKE."

In this instance, looking upon the dying brother as the agent and the sister as the *intended* percipient, the question arises, why was *she* unable to perceive the telepathic influence which presented the likeness of her brother, while the colored nurse, an entire stranger to him, sees and describes him standing by his sister's chair and apparently anxious that she should recognize him?

In another of Mr. Gurney's cases, of four persons

present in a business office where the phantasm of a fifth well-known person appeared, two persons saw the phantasm and two did not.

Abridged from Mr. Gurney's account the circumstances were as follows:—

The narrator is Mr. R. Mouat, of 60 Huntingdon St., Barnsbury, N., and the incident occurred in his office on Thursday, September 5th, 1867. The persons concerned were the Rev. Mr. H., who had a desk in the same office and who may be considered the *agent;* Mr. Mouat, himself, and Mr. R., a gentleman from an office upstairs in the same building, the *percipients;* while a clerk and a porter who were also present saw nothing.

Mr. Mouat goes into his office at 10:45 o'clock on the morning of September 5th, sees his clerk and the porter in conversation, and the Rev. Mr. H. standing at the corner of a table at the back of the clerk. He is about to speak to Mr. H. about his being there so early (more than an hour before his usual time), when the clerk commenced speaking to him about business and especially a telegram concerning which something was amiss. This conversation lasted several minutes and was decidedly animated. During this scene, Mr. R., from an office upstairs, comes in and listens to the excited conversation. He looks at Mr. H. in a comical way, motioning with his head toward the two disputants, as much as to say "they are having it hot;" but to Mr. R.'s disgust Mr. H. does not respond to the joke. Mr. R. and the porter then leave the room. Mr. Mouat turns to Mr. H., who was all the while standing at the corner of the table, notices that he looks downcast, and is without his neck-tie; he says to him, "Well, what is the matter with *you*, you look so sour?" Mr. H. makes no reply, but looks fixedly at Mr. Mouat. Having finished some papers he was reading Mr. Mouat noticed Mr. H. still standing at the table. The clerk at that moment handed Mr. Mouat a letter saying, "Here, sir, is a letter from Mr. H."

No sooner was the name pronounced than Mr. H. disappeared in a second.

Mr. Mouat is dumfounded—so much so that the clerk notices it. It is then discovered that the clerk has not seen Mr. H. at all, and declares that he has not been in the office that morning. The letter from Mr. H. was written on the previous day and informs Mr. Mouat that he is ill, and will not be at the office the next day, and asks to have his letters sent to his house.

The next day, Friday, Mr. H. enters the office at his usual hour, twelve o'clock; and on being asked by Mr. Mouat where he was the previous day at 10:45 o'clock, he replied that at that time he had just finished breakfast—was at home with his wife, and did not leave the house all day.

The following Monday Mr. Mouat meets Mr. R. and asks him if he remembers being in his office the previous Thursday morning. R. replies that he does, perfectly. Does he remember who were present and what was going on? "Yes," said Mr. R., "you were having an animated confab with your clerk about a telegram. Besides yourself and the clerk there were present the porter and Mr. H."

On being informed that Mr. H. was at home, fourteen miles' distant, at that time, Mr. R. became indignant that any one should insinuate that he did not know a man was present when he saw him. He insisted on calling the porter to corroborate him; but on being questioned, the porter, like the clerk, declared that he did not see anything of Mr. H. that morning.

Here, in broad daylight, of four persons present and engaged in business, two saw Mr. H. and addressed him either in words or by signs, while two others with equal opportunities did not see him at all.

The Rev. Mr. H. at home during the time had

no particular experience of any kind. All that can be said is, that, it must have been about his usual time for starting for the office; he had sent a letter about his mail which he knew would then be received, and all the general routine and habit of his life would tend to direct his mind to that locality at that particular time. He was ill as he appeared to be to those who saw his *appearance* at the office, and very likely he was negligently dressed.

Why should two of those present have seen his apparition, and two others have failed to see it? For the simple reason that, as in ordinary thought-transference, or in the "willing game" some are *good subjects*, or percipients, and others are not. For the same reason that of ten persons making trial of Planchette-writing, the board will move for only two or three out of the whole number—that is, in only a few would the hands act automatically in response to a subliminal self; and for the same reason it may also be true that amongst several persons, in only a few of those present, can the sense of sight or hearing be effected by a phantasm.

In many instances, children, and in some instances, very young children, have been the percipients—children too young to perceive any difference between the phantasm and a real person, and who have accordingly addressed it and spoken of it as they would of a real person. Even animals, especially horses and dogs, have given unmistakable evidence—by crouching, trembling, and fright—of perceiving the same phantasms that have been seen by persons who were present with them. The phantom being, so to speak, *in the air*, it is perceived by those whose organization is so adjusted as to make it *impressionable*, and to constitute, to a greater or less degree, what is known as a *sensitive*.

Doubtless, on close examination, it would be found that persons capable of hypnotization, though they may never have been hypnotized, natural somnambulists, persons accustomed to vivid dreaming, reverie, abstraction, and kindred states, in other words, persons in whom the subliminal self sometimes gives indications of independent action, are most likely to have some *marked* psychical experience. It may be only once in a lifetime, and this one instance *may* be the perception of a phantasmal appearance.

In bringing to a close these examples of apparitions, I wish to introduce one which has specially impressed me. It was the experience of a child—it is reported by the percipient herself. The statement is singularly straightforward, and simple; something was done on account of the vision which impressed the circumstance upon others who did not see it, for prompt action founded upon what was seen, saved a life. I give it in the percipient's own words, written to Mr. Gurney. It is from Mrs. Brettany, 2 Eckington Villas, Ashbourne Grove, Dulwich.

She writes:—

"November, 1884.

"When I was a child I had many remarkable experiences of a psychical nature, and which I remember to have looked upon as ordinary and natural at the time.

"On one occasion (I am unable to fix the date, but I must have been about ten years old) I was walking in a country lane at A., the place where my parents then resided. I was reading geometry as I walked along, a subject little likely to produce fancies, or morbid phenomena of any kind, when, in a moment, I saw a bedroom, known as the White Room in my home, and upon the floor lay my mother, to all appearances dead.

"The vision must have remained some minutes, during which time my real surroundings appeared to pale and die out; but as the vision faded actual surroundings came back, at first dimly, and then clearly. I could not doubt that what I had seen was real. So instead of going home, I went at once to the house of our medical man, and found him at home. He at once set out with me for my home, on the way putting questions I could not answer, as my mother was to all appearances well when I left home.

"I led the doctor straight to the White Room, where we found my mother actually lying as in my vision. This was true, even to minute details.

"She had been seized suddenly by an attack of the heart, and would soon have breathed her last but for the doctor's timely arrival. I shall get my father and mother to read this and sign it."

"JEANIE GWYNNE-BRETTANY."

Mrs. Brettany's parents write :—
"We certify that the above is correct."
"S. G. GWYNNE.
"J. W. GWYNNE."

In answer to inquiries, Mrs. Brettany states further:

"The White Room in which I saw my mother, and afterwards actually found her, was out of use. It was unlikely she should be there.

"She was found lying in the attitude in which I had seen her. I found a handkerchief with a lace border beside her on the floor. This I had distinctly noticed in my vision. There were other particulars of coincidenee which I cannot put here."

Mrs. Brettany's father writes further:—

"I distinctly remember being surprised by seeing my daughter in company with the family doctor, outside the door of my residence; and I asked, 'Who is ill?' She replied, 'Mamma.' She led the way at once to the 'White Room,' where we found my wife lying in a swoon on the floor. It was when I asked when she had been taken ill that I found it must have been after my daughter had left the house. None of the servants in the house knew anything of the sudden illness, which our doctor assured me would have been fatal had he not arrived when he did.

"My wife was quite well when I left her in the morning."

"S. G. GWYNNE."

Taking, as we must, the main incidents of this narrative as true, we have either a simple case of clairvoyance on the part of Mrs. Brettany as a child, or else, on the other hand, the subliminal self of the unconscious mother hastened to impress the situation upon the sensitive child, and with the definite good result which is recorded.

CHAPTER XII.

CONCLUSIONS.

IN gathering up the results of these investigations, it must be stated that in showing their relation to science there is no thought of any detraction from the nobility and greatness of scientific labor and achievement in the material world—that is grand almost beyond expression. The attitude of science is conservative, and it is right; but sooner or later it must awake to the fact that here is a new field for investigation which comes strictly within the limits of its aims, and even of its methods. Many individual members of the great body of scientific workers see and know this; gradually the majority will see it.

On the other hand, it must be stated that there is no intention of covering the whole ground of alleged occult psychic phenomena, but only a portion, even of such as relate to our present life. The subject of the return of spirits is untouched; it is only shown that the domain of alleged spiritualistic manifestations is deeply trenched upon by the action of the subliminal self of living people; what lies beyond that is neither affirmed nor denied; it rests upon ground yet to be cleared up and considered; and any facts open to satisfactory investigation are always welcomed by any of the many persons and societies interested in discovering what is true relating to it.

Confining ourselves within the limits assigned, if the series of alleged facts which has been presented in the preceding chapters be true, then we are in the presence of a momentous reality which, for importance and value, has not been exceeded, if, indeed, it has been approached by any of the discoveries of modern times.

But, it may be said, your alleged facts are not new; they are coeval with history, with mythology, with folk-lore, with religion. Granted that the facts are old, that similar ones have been known from very early times, how have these facts been treated by the leaders of thought in the nineteenth century?

That the earth goes round the sun is an old fact, yet it was not made patent and credible, even to the cultivated, much less to the average mind, till recent times. Evolution has been going on since millions of years before the human race came into existence—it is a very ancient fact, yet it is only within the memory of men still living that it has been found out and accepted. So telepathy has existed ever since the race was young, yet few even now know the facts, observations, and experiments upon which its existence is predicated or comprehend either its theories or its importance. The subliminal self has been active in every age of which we have any record. Yet it has never been recognized as forming a part of each and every individual's mental outfit, but its wonderful action has either been discredited altogether, or else has been credited to foreign or supernatural agencies.

But telepathy can no longer be classed with fads and fancies; if not already an accepted fact, it has certainly attained to the dignity of a theory supported by both facts and experiments; a theory which has attracted to its study a large company of competent men in every civilized country.

A theory, no matter in what department of investigation it may be found, whether relating to matter or mind, is strong in proportion to the number of facts which it will bring into line, harmonize and reduce to system. It is that which makes the Nebular Theory of the formation of the planetary system so wonderfully strong; it harmonizes and reduces to system so many known but otherwise unrelated and unsystematized facts; and it is easier to find excuses or form minor theories to account for isolated and apparently erratic facts, like the retrograde motions of the satellites of Uranus and Neptune, than to give up a theory, at once so grand in itself and at the same time harmonizing so many important astronomical phenomena. The same is true of the undulatory theory of light, and again of the theory of evolution, which forty years ago was looked upon as a flimsy hypothesis, but which is now universally accepted as an established truth. Some of the facts are still unclassified and unexplained, yet it so harmonizes in general the facts of the visible world, that instead of a mass of disjointed and heterogeneous objects and phenomena, such as men beheld in nature only a hundred years ago, the arbitrary work of a blind chance or a capricious Creator, we now behold a beautiful and orderly sequence, progression, and unfolding of the natural world according to laws which command our admiration and stimulate our reverence.

Apart from recent studies, exactly the same condition of chaos and confusion exists regarding psychical phenomena as existed concerning the facts in the physical world only a hundred years ago. Nor is it likening great things to small when we compare the nebular hypothesis, or the theory of evolution, conceptions which have educated an age and vastly enlarged the boundary of human thought, to the theory of telepathy and the fact and power of the subliminal self. For if it was important that men should know the laws governing inanimate matter, to comprehend the orbits and motions of the planets; if it developed the understanding to contemplate the grandeur of their movements, the vast spaces which they traverse, and the wonderful speed with which they accomplish their various journeys—if such knowledge has enlarged the capacity of men's minds, given them truer notions of the magnitude of the universe, and grander conceptions of nature and the infinite power and intelligence which pervades and is exhibited in it, is it not equally important and equally improving and practical to study the subtler forces which pervade living organisms, the still finer laws and adjustments which govern the action of mind?

It has been contended by a large and intelligent class of writers, and those who most pride themselves on scientific methods and the infallibility of scientific inductions, that mind is only the product of organization and ceases to have any activity or even existence when the organs through which it usually manifests itself have perished. The general consensus of mankind is a sharp protest against this conclusion—but the experimental proofs have, to many, seemed in favor of this scientific denial;—the healthy brain in general exhibits a healthy mental activity, the diseased or imperfect brain shows impaired mental action, and the disorganized brain simply exhibits no mental activity nor any evidence whatever of the existence of mind. Nevertheless, it is a lame argument; it is simply an attempt to prove a negative.

The healthy rose emits an agreeable odor which our senses appreciate. You may destroy the rose—it does not prove that the fragrance which it emitted does not still exist even though our senses fail to appreciate it.

But experiment and scientific methods have also somewhat to say upon this subject. And first, in August, 1874, twenty-two years ago, at the moment when the materialistic school was at the height of its influence, both the scientific and religious world were brought to a momentary standstill—like a ship under full headway suddenly struck by a tidal wave—when one of the most eminent scientific men of his time, or of any time, standing in his place as president of the foremost scientific association in the world, spoke as follows: "Abandoning all disguise, the confession which I feel bound to make before you is that I prolong the vision backward across the boundary of experimental evidence and discover in matter, which we, in our ignorance, and notwithstanding our professed reverence for its Creator, have hitherto covered with opprobrium, the promise and potency of every form of life."*

On that day the tap-root of materialism was wounded, and materialism itself has been an invalid of increasing languor and desuetude ever since. On the other hand, supernaturalism in every form was left in little better plight.

To thinking men of all classes this bold declaration opened up the grand thought, not new, but newly formulated and endorsed, that as the seed contained all the possibilities of the future plant —the ovum all the possibilities of the future animal, so matter, which had been thought so lightly of, contained within itself the germ, potency, and promise of nature in all her subsequent developments—of the vast universe of suns and systems, planets and satellites, and of every form

---

* Prof. Tyndall's address before the British Association at Belfast, August, 1874.

of life, sensation, and intelligence which in due process of evolution has appeared upon their surfaces. It pointed the way to the thought of an infinite causal energy and intelligence pervading matter and working through nature in all its various grades of life from the first organized cell up to the grandest man. It gave a new meaning to mind in man, as being an individualized portion of that divine potency which ever existed in matter, and which acting through constantly improving and developing organisms, amidst constantly improving environments, at length appeared a differentiated, individualized, seeing, reasoning, knowing, loving spirit.

The mind, then, is of importance. It is no transient visitor which may have made its appearance by chance—a concatenation of coincidences, fortunate or unfortunate, but it is the intelligent tenant and master of a singularly beautiful and complicated house, a house which has been millions upon millions of years in the building, and yet which will be lightly laid aside when it ceases to accommodate and fulfil the needs of its tenant.

Who and what, then, is this lordly tenant whose germ was coeval with matter, whose birth was in the first living cell which appeared upon the planet, whose apprenticeship has been served through every grade of existence from the humble polyp upwards, whose education has been carried on through the brain and organs of every grade of animal life with its countless expedients for existence and enjoyment, until now, as lord of its domain, it looks back upon its long course of development and education, looks about upon its environments and wonders at itself, at what it sees, and at what it prophesies. Truly what is this tenant, what are its powers, and why is it here at all?

These are the questions which it has been the business of the strongest and wisest to discuss, from the time men began to think and record their thoughts until the present time; but how various and unsatisfactory have been the conclusions. The mental philosophers, psychologists, and encyclopedists simply present a chaos of conflicting definitions, principles, and premises, upon none of which are they in full agreement amongst themselves; they are not even agreed regarding the nature of mind—whether it is material or immaterial—how it should be studied, how it is related to the body, indeed whether it is an entity at all, or simply "a series of feelings or possibilities of them"; whether it possesses in-nate ideas or is simply an accretion of experiences. In short, the stock of generally received facts relating to mind has always remained exceedingly small. Psychologists have busied themselves chiefly about its usual and obvious actions, and when in full relation to the body, ignoring all other mental action or arbitrarily excluding it as abnormal and not to be taken into account in the study of normal mind; so with only half the subject under consideration true results could hardly be attained.

Since the organization of the Society for Psychical Research, in 1882, new fields of investigation have been undertaken and the *unusual* phenomena connected with the operations of mind have been systematically studied. A very hasty and imperfect sketch of this study and of the results obtained has been given in the preceding chapters, but for the use here made of these studies in connection with his own observations the writer alone is responsible. In these studies the field of investigation has been greatly extended beyond that examined by the old philosophers and physiologists. Beyond the usual activities in which we constantly see the mind engaged—observation of surroundings made by the senses, memory of them, reasoning about them, and putting them in new combinations in science, literature, or art—new activities have been observed, activities lying entirely outside the old lines, in new and hitherto unexplored fields.

It has been demonstrated by experiment after experiment carefully made by competent persons that sensations, ideas, information, and mental pictures can be transferred from one mind to another without the aid of speech, sight, hearing, touch, or any of the ordinary methods of communicating such information or impressions. That is, Telepathy is a fact, and mind communicates with mind through channels other than the ordinary use of the senses.

It has been demonstrated that in the hypnotic condition, in ordinary somnambulism, in the dreams and vision of ordinary sleep, in reverie, and in various other subjective conditions the mind may perceive scenes and events at the moment transpiring at such a distance away or under such physical conditions as to render it impossible that knowledge of these scenes and events could be obtained by means of the senses acting in their usual manner. That is, mind under some circumstances *sees* without the use of the physical organ of sight.

Again, it has been demonstrated that some persons can voluntarily project the mind—some mind—some centre of intelligence or independent mental activity, clothed in a recognizable form, a distance of one, a hundred, or a thousand miles, and that it can there make itself known and recognized, perform acts, and even carry on a conversation with the person to whom it was sent. That is, mind can *act* at a distance from, and independent of, the physical body and the organs through which it usually manifests itself.

These propositions present an aspect of mind which the authorities in the old fields of psychology have failed to observe or to recognize; or if they have at times caught a glimpse of it they have rather chosen to close their eyes and deny altogether the phenomena which these propositions imply, because they found it was impossible to classify them in their system. It has been to a degree a repetition of the folly exhibited by Galileo's contemporaries and critics, who refused to look through his telescope lest their favorite theories of the universe should be damaged. Nevertheless, this newly studied aspect exists, and is adding greatly to our knowledge of the nature and action of mind.

Still another class of unusual mental phenomena

found in this outlying field of psychology is that known under the general name of automatism; and by this is meant something more than the "unconscious cerebration" and "unconscious muscular action" of the physiologists, and something quite different from that.

There is, first, the class of motor automatisms, including Planchette-writing and other methods of automatic writing, drawing, painting, and kindred performances, also poetical or metrical improvisations, and trance, and so-called inspirational speaking:—Second, there are the sensory automatisms; or such as are manifested by impressions made upon the senses and which are reckoned as hallucinations. The impression of hearing a voice, of feeling a touch, or seeing a vision may be reckoned as examples of this kind of automatism.

No other division of this newly cultivated field presents so many unusual and debatable phenomena. Not only do those modern mysteries, Planchette-writing, trance-speaking, and mediumistic utterances come easily under this class of mental phenomena, but all that vast array of alleged supernatural phenomena which pervades the literature of every nation since the time when men first began to record their experiences. The oracles of the Greeks and Romans, the dæmon of

Socrates, the voices of Joan of Arc, and the widespread custom of divination by means of crystal-gazing in some of its many forms have already been referred to and their relation to automatism or the action of the subliminal self has been noted.

There is still one important class of persons who have wielded an enormous influence upon mankind, an influence in the main wholesome, elevating, and developing, whose relation to automatism demands a passing consideration. I refer to the religious chiefs of the world.

As prominent examples of those founders of religions we will briefly notice Moses, Zoroaster, Mahomet, and Swedenborg. Each either professed himself to be, or his followers have credited him with being, the inspired mouthpiece of the Deity. There can be no doubt in the minds of candid students that each one of these religious leaders was perfectly honest, both as regards his conception of the character and importance of his doctrines and also regarding the method by which he professed to receive them. Each believed that what he taught was ultimate and infallible truth, and was received directly from the Deity. It is evident, however, that from whatever source they were derived the doctrines could not all be ultimate truth, since they were not in harmony amongst themselves; but the authors of them all present their claim to inspiration, and whose claim to accept and whose to reject it is difficult to decide. But accepting the theory that each promulgated the doctrines, theological, cosmological, and ethical, that came to him automatically through the superior perception of the subliminal self, all the phenomena fall into line with the well ascertained action of that subliminal self.

The truth which Moses saw was such as was adapted to his age and the people with whom he had to deal. So there came to his perception not only the sublime laws received at Sinai, but also the particulars regarding the tabernacle and its furnishing—the rings and the curtains, the dishes and spoons and bowls and covers, the rams' skins dyed red, the badgers' skins, and the staves of shittim wood. The same also is true regarding the teachings of Zoroaster.

The splendid results which followed the promulgation of Mahomet's revelation to a few insignificant Arab tribes are proof of its vital germ of truth and of its adaptability to the soil into which it fell. It developed into a civilization from which, at a later period, a benighted and debased Christianity relighted its torch.

Also the teachings of Swedenborg, notwithstanding the apparent egotism of the man and the tiresome verbiage of many of his communications, are elevating and refining in character and useful to those who are attracted to them. That in either case an infinite Deity spoke the commonplace which is attributed to Him in these communications is incredible, but to suppose it all, both the grand and the trivial, the work of the subconscious self of the respective authors is in accordance with what we know of automatism and of the wonderful work of the subliminal self when left free to exercise its highest activities.

Let us examine with some care the history of two examples of unusual or supranormal mental action, the first found in one of the earliest of human records, and reckoned as fully inspired; the other equally unusual occurring within the last half century and making no claim to any supernatural assistance.

The first example is presented in the first chapter of Genesis, and is a clear, connected, and in the main correct, though by no means complete, account of the changing conditions of the earth in the earliest geological periods, and of the appearance in their proper order of the different grades of life upon its surface. That such a written account should have existed three thousand years before any scientifically constructed schedule even of the order in which plants and and animals succeeded each other, much less of the manner in which the earth was prepared for their reception and nurture, is a most remarkable circumstance, regarded either from a literary or a scientific standpoint. It has been criticised for its lack of scientific exactness, and the supposed error of representing light as created before the sun, ignoring the early existence of aquatic life, and similar points. But let us take our stand with the grand old seer, whoever he may have been, whom we know as Moses, who gave to the world this graphic account of the order of creation so many centuries before science had thrown its light upon the condition of the earth in those far-off ages, and let us endeavor to see what his quickened vision enabled him to behold.

The panorama opens and discloses in an hour the grand progressive action of millions upon millions of years.

The first picture represents the created earth covered with water and enveloped in a thick mantle of steaming mist, causing a condition of absolute and impenetrable darkness upon its surface. In the language of the seer, "The earth was without form and void; and darkness was upon the face of the deep." For ages the unbroken ocean which covered the earth was heated by internal fires; the rising vapor as it met the cooler atmosphere above was condensed and fell in one constant downpour of rain. Unceasing, steaming mist, vapor, and rain, wholly impenetrable to light: such were the conditions.

At length, as the cooling process went on, the density of the mists was diminished;—the wonderful fiat went forth, "Let light be."—and light was. But still the mantle hung close upon the unbroken ocean.

The second picture appears. Not only was there light but a firmament—an arch with a clear space underneath it; and it divided the waters which were above it from the waters which were beneath it.

Picture the third. The waters were gathered together and the continents appeared; and the land was covered with verdure—plants and trees, each bearing seed after its kind. Of the inhabitants of the sea the seer had taken no account. It was simply a picture that he saw—a natural, phenomenal representation.

Picture the fourth. The mists and clouds are altogether dispelled. The clear sky appears. The sun comes forth to rule the day—the moon to rule the night. The stars also appear.

Picture the fifth. The lower orders of animals are in full possession of the earth and sea—fish, fowl, and sea-monsters.

Picture the sixth. The higher orders of creation, mammals and man.

Such was the phenomenal aspect of the various epochs of creation roughly outlined, strong, distinct, and in the main true. Not even the scientific critic with his present knowledge could combine more strength and truth, with so few strokes of the brush.

Relieved of the burden of inspiration and the necessity for presenting absolute and unchangeable truth, and presenting the seer as simply telling what he saw, the picture is wonderful, and the telling is most graphic. It needed no deity nor angel to tell it—it was there—and the subliminal self of the seer whose special faculty it was to see, perceived the scene in all its grandeur. He also was the one best fitted to perceive the laws which should make his people great, and describe the forms and ceremonies which should captivate their senses and lead them on to higher intellectual, moral, and ethical development.

Next take the other example. Fifty years ago a young man, not yet twenty years of age, uneducated, a grocer's boy and shoemaker's apprentice, was hypnotized; and it was found that he had a most remarkable mental or psychical constitution. He had most unusual experiences, and presented unusual psychical phenomena which need not be recounted here.

At length it was impressed upon him as it might have been upon Socrates or Joan of Arc, or Swedenborg or Mahomet, that he had a mission and had a message to give to the world. He came from the rural town where he had spent his boyhood to the city of New York and hired a room on a prominent thoroughfare. He then, in his abnormal condition, proceeded to choose those who should be specially associated with him in his work—men of character and ability whom he did not even know in his normal state. First: Three witnesses were chosen who should be fully cognizant of everything relating to the method by which the message or book was produced. Of these one was a clergyman, one a physician, and one an intelligent layman. Second: A scribe qualified to write out the messages as he dictated them, to edit and publish them. Third: A physician to put him into the hypnotic, or as it was then called, the magnetic condition, in which he was to dictate his messages.

The first lecture was given November 28th, 1845, and the last June 21st, 1847. During this time 157 lectures were given, varying in length from forty minutes to four hours, and they were all carefully written out by the scribe. To 140 of these manuscripts were attached 267 names of persons who listened to them and subscribed their names as witnesses at the end of each lecture—to some a single signature was affixed, to some, many. Any person really desirous of knowing the purport of these lectures and the manner of their delivery could be admitted by making application beforehand.

At each sitting the speaker was first put into the deep hypnotic trance in which he was rigid and unconscious; but his sub-conscious or second self was active and lucid, and associated with the principles and knowledge which he needed and which he was to communicate. From this condition he came back to the somnambulic state in which he dictated that which he had acquired in the deep trance, or what he called the "superior condition"; and the transition from one of these states to the other took place many times during each lecture. Such were the conditions under which Andrew Jackson Davis produced the *Principles of Nature—Her Divine Revelation*—a book of nearly 800 pages, divided into three parts:—First, a setting forth of first principles, which served as a philosophical explanation or key to the main work. Second, a cosmogony or description of the method by which the universe came to its present state of development, and third, a statement of the ethical principles upon which society should be based and the practical working of these principles. It assumes to be thoroughly scientific and philosophical. It has literary faults, and there is plenty of opportunity for cavil and scientific fault-finding; but these remarkable facts remain.

A poor boy, thoroughly well known and vouched for by his neighbors for his strict integrity, having had only five months of ordinary district school instruction for his education, having never read a scientific or philosophical book, and not a dozen all told of every kind, having never associated with people of education except in the most casual way, yet in the manner just described he dictated a book containing the outlines of a thoroughly sound and reasonable system of philosophy, theology, and ethics, and a complete system of cosmogony representing the most advanced views in geology, which was then in its infancy—astronomy, chemistry, and other departments of physical science, criticising current scientific opinions, and in points where he differed from these opinions giving full and cogent reason for that difference.

On March 16th, 17th, and 20th, 1846, he announced the fact of the motion of our sun and solar system about a still greater centre, in harmony with the Nebular Hypothesis by which he explained the formation of the whole vast system. He also announced the existence of an eighth and ninth planet, and the apparently abnormal revolution of the satellites of Uranus. Neptune, the eighth planet, had not then been discovered and was not found until six months later. On the 29th of April he announced the discovery and application of diamagnetism by Faraday, concerning which none of his associates had any knowledge, and which I believe had not then been noticed in this country. He gave a distinct and vivid description of the formation of the different bodies constituting the solar system, of the introduction of life upon our planet, and of its evolution from grade to grade from the lowest to the highest—all in minute detail, in general accord with established scientific deduction and in scientific and technical language. In several particulars he differed from the received opinions, and gave his reasons for so doing. No claim was made to inspiration nor to the presentation of absolute or infallible truth, but when hypnotized and in what he termed the "superior condition," his perceptive faculties were vastly increased, and that which he then perceived he made known. He simply gave the truth as he saw it, and he commended it to the judgment and reason of mankind for reception or rejection. In other words, the subliminal self was brought into action by hypnotism, and then by means of its greatly increased perceptive powers he gathered knowledge from various sources quite inaccessible to him in his ordinary state, and seemingly inaccessible also to others.

Concerning the truth or falsity of the revelations beyond what was already known or has since been confirmed by science, I do not assume to pronounce judgment; but that this also, as well as the first chapter of Genesis, from either a literary or scientific standpoint, is one of the most remarkable productions of this or of any age, will not be denied by any competent and candid examiner; while the remarkable character of the book will be still better appreciated when the status of the theory of evolution and of the science of geology fifty years ago is taken into the account.

Here are presented two prominent examples of supranormal mental activity—one in the early ages of man's development, when *everything* was supernatural, the immediate work of a god—the other in man's later development when natural law is found intervening between phenomena and their cause, and when it is found possible for men to comprehend the fact that truth, extraordinary and even that which had previously been unknown or was beyond the reach of the senses in their ordinary state, may nevertheless be discovered or revealed by other means than direct communications from Deity.

It is seen, then, how various and how wonderfully important are the mental phenomena grouped under the general designation of automatism.

Many examples of this and other classes of unusual mental action have been given in previous chapters, not as cumulative evidence of their verity—that would require volumes, but simply to illustrate the subject and give some degree of definiteness to our reasoning regarding them. Not even all the *classes* of facts properly belonging to our subject have here been represented;

but taking them as they have been enumerated and hastily described, they constitute a body of well observed and well authenticated facts and phenomena of undeniable interest, and if received as true their importance is certainly to be compared with the greatest discoveries of modern science. They are, however, the very facts which the science and philosophy of to-day hesitates to accept. The only exception to this statement is found in the treatment lately accorded to hypnotism, which after a hundred years of hesitation, rejection and even ridicule, has at length been definitely received as regards its main facts. It is true, however, that in numerous other instances the evidence regarding unusual mental states and phenomena is equally weighty and unimpeachable; but because these phenomena are unusual, marvelous or seemingly miraculous, belonging to no recognized class of mental action, therefore it is argued, they cannot be genuine; there *must be* some flaw in the evidence and they cannot be accepted.

It is tedious going over the arguments which reduce this mode of reasoning to an absurdity. The same reasoning has been applied to every important discovery in physical science for the past three hundred years; and if it were carried out to its logical conclusions no substantial advance in human knowledge could ever take place, since every discovery or observation of phenomena outside of known laws must on that ground be rejected. And the history of scientific discoveries shows that this has actually been the case. The announcement of the discovery of the movements of the planets around the sun, of the attraction of gravitation, of the identity of lightning with electricity, of the relation and derivation of species in the world of living forms—of the discovery of living toads in geological strata of untold antiquity, and scores of other now accepted facts, were accounted visionary and were received with scoffs and jeers by the accredited leaders of science, because they were outside of any known natural laws; and it was only after the study and contemplation of the new discoveries had educated and enlarged the minds of a new generation of men to a better understanding of the extent and magnitude of nature and her laws that the scoffs subsided and the new facts quietly took their places as accredited science.

The same process is going on regarding mental phenomena to-day. It may require a generation for men unused to think in this direction to become familiarized with the thought that telepathy, clairvoyance, and the subliminal self, with its augmented powers, are facts in nature; but thousands of intelligent people, and many accustomed to examine facts critically and according to approved methods, are already so interpreting nature, and their number is constantly increasing.

Such are some of the facts discovered by the pioneers in this outlying field of psychology. In attempting to explain or account for them it is useless to take refuge in the hazy definitions of the old psychologists, or to imagine that the secret is bound up in the vital processes which occupy the biologist and physiologist, interesting and important as those studies are; even the neurologist can help us comparatively little—he can tell us all about diseases of the nervous system and how they manifest themselves, and his labor has earned for him the gratitude of mankind; but he cannot tell us how thinking is accomplished, nor what thought is; he cannot tell the cause of so normal and easily observed a phenomenon as ordinary sleep, much less of the new faculties which are developed in somnambulism. In all these related departments of science, in considering mental phenomena it is found convenient to deny the existence of that for which they cannot account. Nature's processes, however, are simple when once we comprehend them, so much so that we wonder at their simplicity, and wonder that we ever could have failed to understand them; and we learn to distrust explanations which are involved and complicated, knowing that error often lies that way. And of this kind for the most part, the attempted explanations of mental processes in terms of physiology have proved to be; they are complicated, inapplicable, and unsatisfactory; and they give no aid in the generalizations which have hitherto been so much needed.

The phenomena in this new field at first sight seem heterogeneous, without system or any common bond; they seem each to demand a separate origin and field. But let the idea of the subliminal self, intelligent, and endowed with its higher perceptive faculties, be presented, and lo! all these refractory phenomena fall into place in one harmonious system. The subliminal self is the active and efficient agent in telepathy—it is that which sees and hears and acts far away from the body, and reports the knowledge which it gains to the ordinary senses, sometimes by motor and sometimes by sensory automatism—by automatic writing, speaking, audition, the vision, the phantasm. It acts sometimes while the primary self is fully conscious—better and most frequently in reverie, in dreams, in somnambulism, but best of all when the ordinary self is altogether subjective and the body silent, inactive, and insensible, as in that strange condition which accompanies the higher phases of trance and lucidity, into which few enter, either spontaneously or by the aid of hypnotism. Then still retaining its attenuated vital connection, it goes forth and sees with extended vision and gathers truth from a thousand various and hidden sources.

Will it act less freely, less intelligently, with less consciousness and individuality when that attenuated vital connection is severed, and the body lies—untenanted?

THE END.

INDEX.

A.

	PAGE
A., Miss, Perceives an induced phantom	236
A., Miss, Her journey automatically described	188
A. B., Clairvoyance of	102–105
Alexis, "	86–87
Anæsthesia, local, produced by hypnotism	67
Apollonius, Clairvoyance of	80
Apparitions or Phantasms, Collective Cases, 293, 294, 295, 299
Automatism	151
" Ancient and modern	331
" Grades or kinds of	151–154
" Motor and sensory	198, 319
Automatisms, Sensory, considered as hallucinations	219
" " manifested by hearing	220
" The dæmon of Socrates	220
" Voices and visions of Joan of Arc	221
Automatic writing, by Planchette	158, 180
" " Mr. W. T. Stead	186–193
" drawing and painting by Mrs. Burton	194
Aylesbury, Commander T. W., Case by	289

B.

B., Madame, Hypnotic subject	58–61, 131–135, 183
Barrett, Prof. W. T., and the S. P. R.	5
Bernheim, Prof., His theories of hypnotism	36
" " Post hypnotic suggestions, cases	63–67
Bishop, The mind-reader	8
Bourne, Ansel, Double personality of	119, 182
Borderland cases. Between sleeping and waking	269

	PAGE
Borderland cases—visions	269, 271, 273
Braid, His theory of hypnotism	31
Brettany, Mrs., Vision, percipient awake	304
Brittan, Dr. S. B., Cases reported by	99–101
Brown, A. J., A second personality	119, 182
Brougham, Lord, Borderland case	273–279
Buchanan, Dr. W. B., Case by, collective	295
Burton, Mrs. Julietta T., Automatic writing	194
" " " Drawing and painting by	195
" " " Portrait, by (Frontispiece)	196
" " " Psychometric powers	199

C.

Carpenter, Dr. Wm. B., His theory	9
Charcot, Prof., His theory of hypnotism	33
Chiefs, Religious	320
" " Moses, Zoroaster, Mahomet, Swedenborg	320
Clairvoyance	74
" Instances of	78–109
" Ancient and modern	81
" Nature of	109
Cleave, Mr. A. H. W., and Mr. H. P. Sparks, Phantasm produced by	234
Clerke, May, Case reported by	296
Collyer, Dr. R. H., Case, vision, reported by	285, 288
Coues, Dr. E., Case reported by	88–90
Crystal-gazing, Used for producing visions	200
" " Cases reported by Mr. E. W. Lane	201
" " Practised in all ages	203
" " Amongst the Hebrews	204
" " " " Greeks	205
" " In the Opera of Parsifal	206
" " The Shew-stone of Dr. Dee	204
" " What it really is	208
" " Experiments of Miss X	209–214
" " Col. Wickham's pouch-belt found by	214

INDEX. 339

	PAGE
Crystal-gazing, Springs and wells used for	216
Cumberland, Mind-reader	8

D.

Davis, A. J., Production of *Principles of Nature, Her Divine Revelation*, by	328
Deyer, Col. J. J., His well, in relation to Crystal-gazing	216
Diagrams, Illustrating thought-transference	19
Dreams, Definite impressions during	263
" Veridical, cases of	263, 266
Dufay, Dr., Case reported by	95

E.

Elliotson, Dr., Mesmeric treatment by	43

F.

Fenton, Mr. F. D., Vision, case reported by	284
Fitzgerald, John, Clairvoyance of	101

G.

Gerault, Dr., Clairvoyance, case reported by	95
Gibert, Dr., Experiments, hypnotizing at a distance	59
Ghost-stories, Status of	1
Glissoid, Mr. E. M., Hypnotic experiments by	231
Gurney, Mr. E., Experiments	21
" " Cases reported, 263–266, 284–289, 291–294, 295,	299
Gurwood, John, His supposed spirit	170
" " His crest	171
" " In the Peninsular War	173
Guthrie, Malcolm, Experiments in Thought-Transference	18

H.

Hammond, Dr. Wm. A., Experiments reported by	56
Harris, Surgeon, A child's vision, case reported	282
Hauffé, Madame, The Seeress of Proverst	83–86
Hodgson, Dr. Richard, Case reported by	122

INDEX.

	PAGE
Hosmer, Harriet, Borderland case	271
Hypnotism, In literature	2
" Historical sketch of	28
" Braid's theory of	31
" Mesmer's theory of	29
" Charcot's theory of	33
" Bernheim's theory of	36–39
" Stages of	41, 51, 52
" Therapeutic effects of	42–50
" Psychic aspect of	51–71
" Rapport in	54
" Suggestion in	61–67
Hypnotizing at a distance	57
" " " Experiments by Prof. Janet and Dr. Gibert	58
" " " Experiments by Prof. Richet and Dr. Héricourt	60

I.

Individual, The, Conception of 149

J.

James, Prof., Case examined by 122
Jane, Clairvoyance of 90–94
Janet, Prof., Hypnotizing at a distance 60
" " Hypnotic experiments by 131
Joan of Arc, Her voices and visions 221
Joy, Mr. A., Case hallucination affecting sight, hearing and touch 291

L.

L. A. W., Remarkable dream or vision 263
Léonie, Léontine, Léonore 131–135
Liébeault, Dr., Suggestion fulfilled after many days ... 63
" " Suggests a disappearance 66
Lucidity, See Clairvoyance.

M.

"Marie," Clairvoyance of 95–99

INDEX.

	PAGE
Mesmer, Anton	29
Mesmerists, The early	31
Mesmerization of inanimate objects	69
Magnetized water, Detection of	71, 215
M. L., Clairvoyance of	105–108
Moses, The vision of	323
Mouat, Mr. R., Narrates a case, phantasms	299
Myers, Mr. F. W. H., His important work	145
" " " Cases examined and reported by,	91, 124, 164, 214

N.

Newnham, Rev. Mr. and Mrs., Planchette writing.. 164–168

O.

Oracles, Greek.. 79

P.

Perception, Definition of	225
Perceptions, which are reckoned as hallucinations	226
Personality, Double or multiplex	116
" " " cases of	117, 124–128
" " " in dreaming	141
Phantasms of the Living, Cases from	231, 263, 289
" Produced at a distance, case	234–238
" Collective cases	293, 294, 295–299
Phenomena, Psychical, Compared with physical	311
Planchette	154–180
Podmore, Mr. F., Case by	288
Psychical Research, Eng. Society for, established	3
Puysegur, Marquis de	30

R.

R., Miss, and Miss V., Planchette writing	168
Rapport, Hypnotic, Example	56
" " Experiments by Mr. Gurney and Dr. Myers	56
" " Experiments by Dr. Hammond	56
" " At a distance	57

	PAGE
Reed, On Personality	116
Revelation, A modern	327
Richardson, Mrs. M. A., Borderland case reported by	269
Russell, Mrs. J. M., Case by	246–248
Ruth, Mrs. Wickham's servant, Crystal-gazing	214

S.

Sidgwick, Prof. H., Vice-Pres. S. P. R	5
" Mrs. H., Cases reported by	88–94
Society for Psychical Research, formation of	3–5, 316
Socrates, Dæmon of	220
Somnambulism	129
" Hypnotic	131
Stainton, Moses, Rev. W., Phantoms perceived by	237, 238
Stead, W. T., His automatic writing	186
" " Miss A.'s journey automatically described by	188
" " Needs of a stranger written out by	189
" " His correspondent in a railway car	192
Stewart, Prof. Balfour	5
Subliminal self, The key to many psychical phenomena	260
" " Sources of information of	177
" " Theory of	257
Suggestion, Post-hypnotic	61
Smith, J. W., and Kate, Experiments	22
Swedenborg, Clairvoyance of	81–83

T.

Telepathy, Theories regarding	250–261
" Explained by the action of the subliminal self	257–261
" No longer a mere fancy	309
Thought-transference, First report on	6
" " Classification	11
" " Experiments by diagrams	18
" " Tested by taste	21
" " " objects	13
" " " cards	13

INDEX. 343

	PAGE
Thought-transference, Tested by fictitious names	14
" " " two percipients	23, 24
Tyndall, Prof., His Belfast address, effect of	312–313

U.

Urim and Thummim, A method of Crystal-gazing..... 204

V.

V., Louis, Case of 124
V., Miss, Planchette writing by 159–164
Verity, The Misses, perceive induced phantasms... 239–244
Visions, Percipient being awake.............................. 282
   " Cases................ 282, 284–286, 289–291, 304
Voisin, Dr., Cases reported by...................... 124, 148

W.

Water, magnetized, detected by patients............ 71, 77
Wedgwood, Mr. H., Planchette-writing............ 168–174
Willing game... 6
Wyld, Dr., Case reported by..................................... 294

X.

X., Case illustrating sensory automatism.............. 184
X., Félida, Case, double personality................ 117–119
X. Miss., On Crystal-gazing............................ 209

Y.

Young, Dr. A. K., Remarkable dream or vision....... 266

Z.

Z., Alma, Case of... 125
Zoist, The, Report of cases in........................... 42

www.ingramcontent.com/pod-product-compliance
Lightning Source LLC
Chambersburg PA
CBHW011958150426
43201CB00018B/2325